AMERICA³

The Women's Team

SBYC

AMERICA³

The Women's Team

by
PAUL LARSEN

Photographs by
DANIEL FORSTER

LEGACY BOOKS

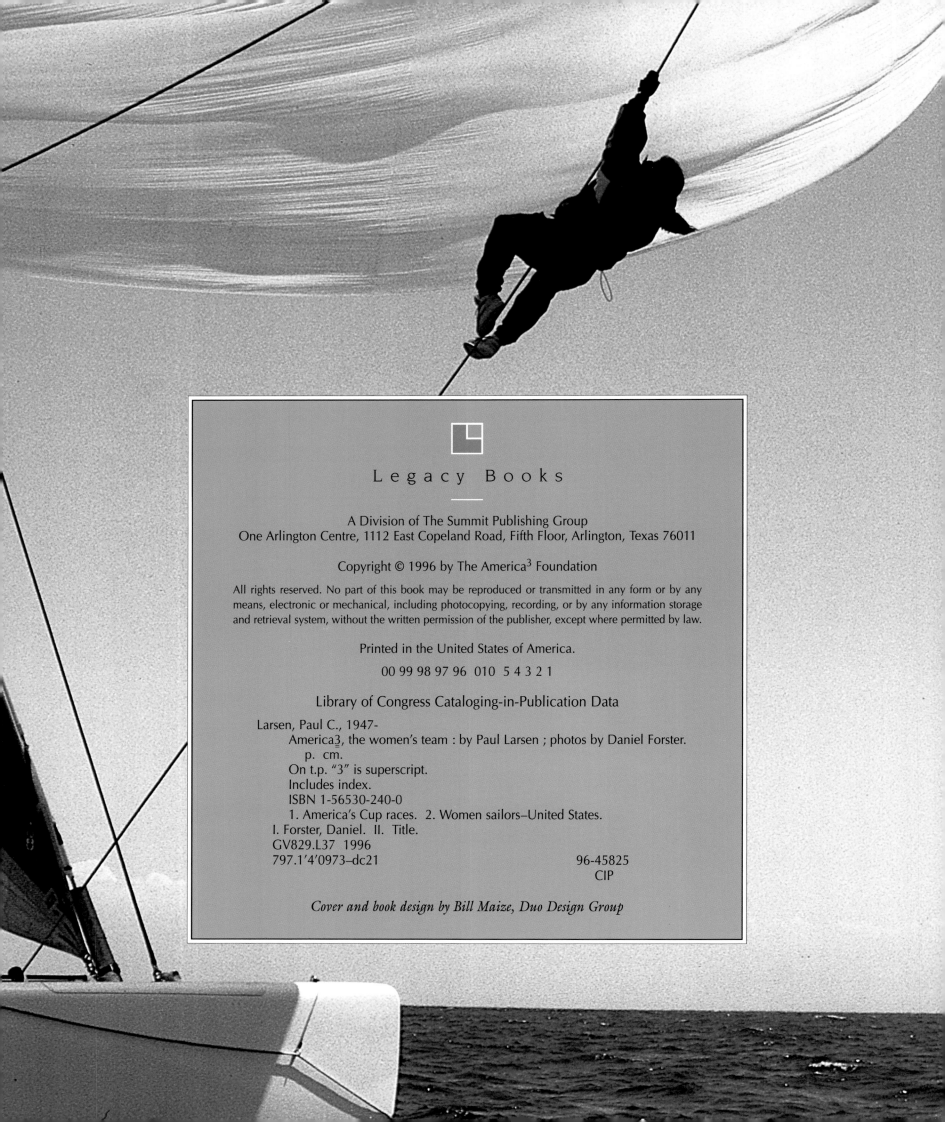

Legacy Books

A Division of The Summit Publishing Group
One Arlington Centre, 1112 East Copeland Road, Fifth Floor, Arlington, Texas 76011

Printed in the United States of America.

00 99 98 97 96   010   5 4 3 2 1

Library of Congress Cataloging-in-Publication Data

Larsen, Paul C., 1947-
    America3, the women's team : by Paul Larsen ; photos by Daniel Forster.
        p. cm.
    On t.p. "3" is superscript.
    Includes index.
    ISBN 1-56530-240-0
    1. America's Cup races. 2. Women sailors–United States.
    I. Forster, Daniel. II. Title.
    GV829.L37 1996
    797.1'4'0973–dc21   96-45825
                                                           CIP

Cover and book design by Bill Maize, Duo Design Group

This book is dedicated

with my grateful thanks to all the men and women

whose valiant effort on the 1995 America³ Women's Team

once again proved that ordinary people can do extraordinary things

with the right combination of teamwork, technology, and talent.

Like most pioneers throughout history,

your accomplishments will be recognized

for years to come.

Bill Koch

Bill Koch, who made the women's team possible, was never shy about expressing his views on the team's abilities.

THE IDEA

During the spring and summer of 1995 when the America's Cup defense trials were the focus of the sailing world, a television advertisement for Chevrolet was aired picturing a number of the women sailors on the America[3] team. The ad attracted viewers' attention because of its stark, black and white images and its tag line: "Proud to be a part of the changing face of sailing."

In the minute or so that the ad filled TV screens across the country, a powerful statement was made—actually, two. One was that the sport of sailing was changing dramatically because of the inclusion of a women's team in the 144-year-old competition for the oldest trophy in sports, a competition formerly dominated by male teams. The second was that one of the biggest corporations in America had chosen both to sponsor the women's team and to use it in the attempt to sell its cars and trucks. While this was by no means the first time the female form had been used by Madison Avenue to sell products, it may have been the first time an entire team of women athletes had been judged an attractive, persuasive marketing tool.

Like so many great ideas, the original author of this one will perhaps forever be lost to obscurity. Bill Koch, who made the dream a reality, is the first to say that the concept of a women's team competing for the America's Cup was not his. Nor was it particularly recent. More than twenty-five years ago, a fledgling Cup group in Connecticut attempted to raise funds for an all-female team. Since then, the idea had been periodically revived as women sailors became more numerous and more prominent; but until 1995, the idea remained just that—an idea.

Only three women had been known to sail in actual Cup matches. The former Hope Goddard, married to C. Oliver Iselin, was aboard *Defender* in 1895, *Columbia* in 1899, and *Reliance* in 1903. All three boats were successful in defending the Cup. Mr. Iselin was one of the syndicate managers of these three defender groups, but it is not recorded whether Mrs. Iselin had an official position, although it is suspected she was the timekeeper.

The position of timekeeper was quite important during this era of the giant sloops, when the yachts measured from 123 feet to 143 feet. Unlike today's boats, which place a premium on maneuverability, easy mobility was not a dominant characteristic of the older yachts. Timed starts were the rule. Because it would take forty seconds or more to jibe these large craft, timing prestart maneuvers was crucial to the helmsman deciding when to turn for the starting line.

Both of the other women who raced in America's Cup matches did hold the position of timekeeper. Phyllis Brodie Gordon, married to Thomas Octave Murdock Sopwith, the famous British aircraft manufacturer, raced with her husband aboard *Endeavour* in 1934 and *Endeavour II* in 1937. Mrs. Sopwith had a high profile as timekeeper and made numerous public appearances. She was photographed many times with stopwatch in hand, and her image graces a number of historical accounts of the races against *Rainbow* ('34) and *Ranger* ('37).

Aboard the victorious defenders *Rainbow* and *Ranger* was Gertrude ("Gertie") Vanderbilt, wife of helmsman Harold S. Vanderbilt, thus setting up the only time in history that two women competed against each other in Cup matches. Also in *Ranger*'s afterguard were three illustrious sailors who in later years had a major impact on sailing and the

Cup: Rod Stephens, Olin Stephens, and Arthur Knapp.

Although no other women have raced in the America's Cup finals, there have been four women who played prominent roles aboard Cup boats during racing in the defender trials. Sis Morrs Hovey raced on *Yankee* in its unsuccessful attempt to become the defender in 1934.

Christy Steinman Crawford, of San Diego, was the back-up navigator in Dennis Conner's 1980 and 1983 efforts. Conner also employed a woman as backup navigator in his 1986-87 campaign when he won the Cup back from the Australians. She was Dory Vogel, of Newport, Rhode Island. Mrs. Vogel's husband, Scotty, was bowman aboard *Stars & Stripes*.

Dawn Riley from Detroit competed in the 1992 defender trials as pitman in the America[3] campaign. One of the top sailors in

When the new team was formed, it had use of 1992 America's Cup champion America[3] *and her stablemate* Kanza.

In one of the most-published photos of the 1995 America's Cup, Bill Koch gets carried away during a sponsor's press conference in San Diego.

the world, she gained renown on the British women's crew in the grueling Whitbread 'Round the World Race in 1989-90, in which her boat *Maiden* came in second.

The genesis of the 1995 America³ team can probably be tracked to the words of a five-year-old boy. After the America³ syndicate had won the 1992 America's Cup in an unprecedented first effort, the team's founder and skipper, Bill Koch, was asked if he would launch a campaign for the next Cup. Bill told the reporter to ask his son, Wyatt, who sat on his father's lap. The reporter asked. "No!" was the answer. The reporter wanted to know why not. "Because it takes too long" were the words that may have changed sporting history.

Bill Koch had thrown himself into winning the twenty-eighth edition of sailing's most prestigious event with his heart, soul, and bank account. But to his mind what cost him

the most was the time away from his son, and he promised Wyatt that would not happen again. Furthermore, he had nothing left to prove. What would be his incentive to enter the 1995 America's Cup?

Yet, if the reigning champion wasn't going to be involved, what would become of his team and its assets? There was the proven fastest International America's Cup Class (IACC) boat in the world, *America³*, and her stablemate, *Kanza*. There were millions of dollars in sails and equipment. And most of all, there were the data banks of state-of-the-art technology that had resulted from years of scientific research.

The man who confounded yachting traditionalists with his highly technical and somewhat unconventional approach to sailboat racing and team management was sitting on a motherlode of machinery and information.

And everyone else still in the game wanted it. But selling or giving it away didn't seem right to Koch, so the question remained for more than a year—what should he do with it?

The answer began to form in the early part of 1993. Koch had already been contacted on two occasions by The Pegasus Group regarding possible support of their women's team concept, but he eventually decided to establish his own team. The idea intrigued him for a number of reasons. Because he would not be as totally immersed in all aspects of the campaign as he was in 1992, he could keep his hand in the event without breaking his promise

to Wyatt. A market survey of the America's Cup he commissioned after 1992 showed that the regatta needed to enhance its image and broaden its interest. A team of women battling teams of men in head-to-head competition, the only such contest in a major, international sport, should accomplish both objectives. And there was the sociopolitical factor: Here was a chance to break barriers, shatter myths, and create opportunities. The idea also appealed to him on a personal level—His mother, Mary, had been a first-rate sportswoman who was athletically equal, if not superior, to many men of her era in tennis, golf, fishing, and hunting.

As the idea gained momentum, a new name, a new management team, and a core group of women were selected to form the nucleus of a syndicate that was originally designed to be the successor to America[3]. In early September of 1993, a small group of men and women met on Cape Cod, Massachusetts, to prepare for the announcement of a women's team to challenge for the America's Cup in less than fifteen months.

The team would be known as "4America," and it would have access to the assets of America[3]. It was to also be managed under the same principles that guided the 1992 team to victory. Chief among those principles was Bill Koch's belief that the team was the only star; no individual agendas were to be accepted. The tenets on which the 1992 team had built success—teamwork, talent, and technology—were still in place. And, since equality was one of the messages of the team's formation, it was established that the athletes who had been asked to the meeting would be invited to try out for the team. Although their proven skills and abilities were the reason for their presence at the meeting, no one had yet won a place on the team.

Through the weekend, the group met to plan things such as where and when the team announcement would be made, how to answer media questions, even whether "helmsman" or "helmswoman" was correct usage ("helmsman" was the consensus).

However, things didn't work out as planned. A difference of opinion over a number of issues arose between Koch and members of the new management team and the America[3] leader decided to make a change. In fact, the whole idea of a women's team supported by America[3] was in jeopardy for some time.

But in the end, it was just too strong an idea—an idea whose time had come. Koch decided that he had to act. Let's run this in-house, he reasoned. Not only was he in possession of the many assets that contributed to the '92 victory, but most of the management team was still in place. It was a logical move to bring in Vincent Moeyersoms as president of America[3] to direct all operations. A recent recipient of an M.B.A., he was ready to put theory into practice.

Born in Belgium and trained in physics, his scientific background and love of sailing had served him well in Koch's employ for more than a decade. As the chief operating officer and executive vice president of the 1992 team, Moeyersoms acted as the coordinator of design, technical research, construction, sail development, instrumentation, shore operations, coaching, tenders, and scheduling. Little happened during the complex preparation of the team and the boats without his knowledge or approval. While managing the women's

Vincent Moeyersoms was selected to direct all operations, a position he was well suited for after his experience as chief operating officer of the 1992 campaign.

team would be anything but routine, it did seem to fit well within his recent experience.

With Moeyersoms in charge, Koch's confidence in the idea began to grow once again. Early confidential feelers to potential sponsors were met with positive enthusiasm. Negotiations with the San Diego Yacht Club, the current custodian of the America's Cup and the defending club of record, were going well. Two other defending syndicates had previously announced their intentions, and sponsorship programs already in place called for funds to be disbursed to the Stars & Stripes and PACT '95 campaigns. America[3] wanted, and was given, a share. The club, Dennis Conner (boss of Stars & Stripes), and PACT '95 officials all privately endorsed the idea. All that was left was to finalize the core team and make the announcement publicly.

The core team had increased in number from those attending the September 1993 meeting on Cape Cod. Between then and the first months of 1994, nine women athletes had

Site of the historic women's team announcement, New York's Plaza Hotel was a majestic backdrop to 1992 Cup racer Defiant.

The announcement was witnessed by a room full of journalists, sailors, potential sponsors, and interested spectators. News of the unprecedented team generated worldwide headlines and more media coverage than all preceding America's Cups combined.

been invited to try out for the team. Six of them were world-class sailors, the other three were Olympic rowers. Together, they had collected enough gold and silver to bankroll most emerging countries. Yet, despite their impressive credentials, it was continuously stressed that no one had made the team; each woman would have to prove herself before the eyes of the A³ coaches. And just as pure talent had taken a backseat to teamwork in the '92 campaign, so, too, did the principle of working together outweigh previous accomplishments during the tryout period for the '95 team. Of the nine women who were introduced to the world as the core team, only six were on the final roster, and of those, only three regularly sailed in Cup races.

While such statistics don't tell the whole story, they do indicate the strength of the female talent pool in the sport. In fact, although America³ management expected competition for team positions to be stiff, they were overwhelmed by both the interest generated and the quality of the applicants. From day one, skill and ability were never in question. The only factor to success that left the

media and public wondering was experience, and providing that was one of the major reasons the team was formed.

On the last day of February, 1994, a tractor trailer, two cars, one man, two women, and a dog left Sparks, Nevada, headed for New York City with a rather unusual cargo. Strapped to the bed of the tractor trailer was the seventy-five-foot IACC sailboat called *Defiant*, a veteran of the 1992 America's Cup battles. The second of four boats built by America³, she had been undefeated in her first six races and won eleven total before her retirement. In nine days' time the boat would receive a police escort in front of somewhat startled New Yorkers as she made her way down Manhattan streets to the Plaza Hotel, the scene of the historic announcement.

Although the name of the boat and the implications of the announcement were mere coincidence, it was no secret that Koch had had his battles with Cup organizers over how to publicize the event. Following his 1992 victory, the defending champion had made a number of suggestions to Cup powers-that-be. Few were given much consideration.

The America³ compound was a state-of-the-art sailboat racing and office complex that served as home to the women's team for almost a year.

But it was history, not politics, that was the order of the day on March 9 when Bill Koch walked to the podium in a room filled with journalists, sailors, potential sponsors, and interested spectators. As flashbulbs popped and news cameras whirled, Koch told the crowd, "America³ will field an all-female team in the 1995 America's Cup...We proved in 1992 that with the right attitude, teamwork, and talent, ordinary people can do extraordinary things. Our goal is to empower women with this same formula for success and take the America³ women's team all the way to victory in 1995."

Anticipating the discussion of the issue that was probably debated more than any other in the months following the announcement, Koch addressed the question of physical strength. "Fifty-five percent of America's Cup success is boat speed," said the man with three degrees from M.I.T. "Twenty percent is tactics, 20 percent is crew work, and 5 percent is luck. Of the crew work, only 10 percent can be measured in strength, which is only 2 percent of the entire equation."

And so the idea that had been voiced more than a quarter century ago had now become a reality. A women's team would compete against men for the America's Cup. David Dellenbaugh, who was the starting helmsman and tactician aboard the *America³* boat in '92, perhaps best summed up how the idea would take form. "What you're going to see in the next year is unlike anything that you've ever seen: a team of women competing with men at the top level of an international sport. That idea is unique. It's exciting. It'll attract a lot of attention and it will make history. The impact of all that will be great for women. It'll be great for sport. It'll be great for sailing and it'll be great for all the sponsors who choose to come on board."

While the announcement itself and the women on the core team were the stars of the day, a list of prominent individuals who would serve on the board of advisors was made public. Tapping the fields of sports, entertainment, business, science, and philanthropy, the A³ managers had assembled a group of sixteen men and women that included sports commentator Donna de Varona, American Red Cross president Elizabeth Dole, former First Lady Betty Ford, actress Whoopi Goldberg, former Olympian Rafer Johnson, actor Cliff Robertson, and pioneer aviator Jeana Yeager.

If such an impressive list of high achievers agreeing to lend their names and time to the team was not enough to convince skeptics of the seriousness of this syndicate, Koch's statement that he would provide several million dollars of seed money undoubtedly left few really believing this was merely a publicity stunt. With a budget of $20 million, the idea

that had enticed many for so long had finally become a reality.

It was a bold statement that seemed at once ahead of its time and too late in coming. At the end of the twentieth century—after this country and the world had been through so many social and political "revolutions"—the statement not only confirmed the reality of changes already made, but was also a visionary look to the future. Whether an all-female team would indeed break barriers, shatter myths, and create opportunities in the stodgy, blue-blazer world of yacht racing perhaps would not be evident for years to come, but Koch was well aware that the future is built on the past. Coincidentally, the announcement was made during Women's History Month.

Among the prominent individuals who served on the team's Board of Advisors were (front row, left to right): Jeana Yeager, Gloria Allred, Joan Finney, Cliff Robertson, Susan Blakely, Donna de Varona, Mary Frances Penny Wagley, and Thor Ramsing (who served on the A³ Board of Directors).

A bird's eye view of the team in position while training before competition began. Although women had little experience aboard IACC boats prior to this effort, the America³ team proved they were highly coachable and very quick to learn.

*T*HE TEAM

In addition to the nine women who had been selected as the core team, Koch also introduced members of the executive, operations, technology and design, marketing, and communications staffs. Of the seventeen people listed in the original press kit as members of those staffs, only four of them had not been a part of the 1992 effort. It was clear that while Koch would not be involved on a day-to-day basis, he was putting the full power of the formidable team that had won the America's Cup behind this campaign. It was a statement that the all-women's team was not some gimmick.

"It's very serious," said Koch. "We think that with the right focus, attitude, dedication, fast boats, and infrastructure, they cannot only compete with the very best in the world in a man's sport...but they can also win."

Joining Koch and Moeyersoms on the executive staff were Rick Wrightson and Brad Robinson. Wrightson is a native Californian who sailed aboard Koch's famous maxi-boats *Matador* and *Matador*[2] for eight years, including six Maxi World Championships. He handled a number of business and finance matters in the '92 campaign and had signed on this time as vice president and deputy chief operating officer in charge of private fund-raising.

Robinson had been involved with the America[3] Foundation and Koch's company, the Oxbow Corporation, since 1989. He would assume corporate legal, tax, financial, and general business responsibilities for the newly-formed team.

Four men who played significant roles on the 1992 team made up the "operations" staff. As director of sailing operations, James (Kimo) Worthington was handed the responsibility of designing and implementing a program which would prepare a mostly inexperienced sailing team for the most experience-needed regatta in the world. His first America's Cup had been aboard *Clipper* in 1980 and, seven years later, he was the mainsheet trimmer on *Eagle*. As alternate helmsman, tactician, crew boss, boat captain, and mainsheet trimmer on the 1992 A[3] team, Kimo had the opportunity to display his sailing knowledge and skills, which led to his position on the new team.

Kimo was aided by a number of sailors who brought a mixture of abilities and expertise to the team. Chief among them was the legendary Buddy Melges, who was officially listed as "special consultant and coach." His illustrious racing career includes more than sixty major national and international sailing championships, and when he was hired for his new assignment, he was the only sailor in the

Brad Robinson handled a number of legal and financial matters for the '92 and '95 teams.

(above right) Rick Wrightson served on the executive staffs of the 1992 and 1995 campaigns.

"Kimo" Worthington, director of sailing operations, designed and implemented a program that taught fundamentals and prepared the team for battle.

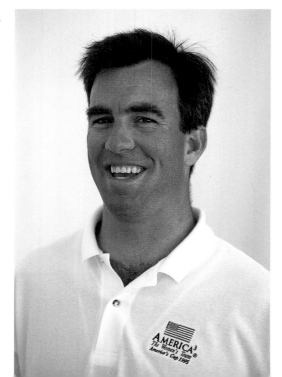

world to have won an Olympic gold medal (1972) and been a helmsman aboard an America's Cup winner (*America*^{3} in 1992). Known in the sailing world as "The Wizard of Zenda," Melges is the founder and chairman of Melges Boat Works in Zenda, Wisconsin. As Buddy likes to say, "Zenda is not the end of the earth...but you can see it from there."

Sharing the same title as Buddy was Dellenbaugh, who, in addition to articulating the attributes of the team at the New York announcement, brought to this new campaign one of the best tactical minds in the country, as well as a precise understanding of the racing rules. Dellenbaugh had raced with Melges in previous America's Cups aboard *Heart of America* in 1987 and again aboard *America*^{3}. His soft-spoken approach to coaching and his ability to teach sailing fundamentals in an informative and thorough manner had earned him the respect of his students through the years. His temperament and personality were perfectly suited to his new position.

Completing the operations staff was Peter Grubb, the director of compound operations. Grubb had served as captain of Koch's two eighty-five-foot maxis, *Matador* and *Matador*^{2}, as well as overseeing the construction of *Jayhawk* and the maintenance of *Defiant, Kanza,* and *America*^{3} in '92. The compound located at 4960 North Harbor Drive on San Diego's inner harbor had gone through a number of physical changes and legal complications following the 1992 Cup. By the time the new team was ready to use it for the next campaign, it had suffered the ravages of vandals and court hearings, which ran the gamut from a claim for money owed America[3] for improvements made, to a claim of ownership by a squatter. Grubb and his team had their hands full reconditioning the

Buddy Melges, co-helmsman of the 1992 Cup winner, brought his coaching skills and legendary storytelling abilities to the 1995 team.

Orginally signed on as a coach, David Dellenbaugh (here receiving a hug from JJ Isler) later found that his tactical expertise and experience were needed on board.

Peter Grubb (left) was a vice president and director of compound operations at the North Harbor Drive facility. Erick Soper (right) headed the shore crew and was also a key member of the 1992 A³ team.

Head of security, former professional football player Marty Stephan spoke softly and carried a big stick.

area and building what amounted to a new complex. Time was short, but they somehow managed.

Carved out of a dilapidated dock area in 1991, the A³ compound was a state-of-the-art boat-racing facility and office complex that would function more as home than apartment over the next year for the team. On the grounds, a machine shop, rigging loft, lami-

nating shop, sail loft, winch shed, woodworking area, dry dock, travel lift, lifting crane, and dock area served as "offices" for Grubb's crew. All was protected by an electronic surveillance system under the management of security chief Marty Stephan, a former professional football player and grinder on the '92 A³ team. Stephan, whose powerful body and gentle voice portrayed a contradiction of tough guy/soft guy, was a favorite of the women sailors.

After the March 9 announcement, frenetic activity began at the compound. The first team tryout was scheduled for mid-April, which meant that the area had to be at least partially renovated in about one month's time. And to have boats for the tryouts, the two IACC boats *America³* and *Kanza*, the last two of the four boats built for the '92 campaign, had to be brought to San Diego from their Nevada dry dock and rerigged for racing.

The first women to arrive in San Diego were Diana Klybert, Lisa Charles, Jane Oetking, and Melissa Purdy. Although all were sailors, they were actually asked to come to help refurbish the compound and prepare the boats. In return, they would have the opportunity to try out for the team and they would also have the advantage of being the first to display their skills and attitude. No promises were made or implied. So, with chainsaw and ditty bag in hand, the four worked alongside a crew of men to prepare for the first tryout session.

Klybert had come to sailing late in her life compared to most America's Cup sailors, taking up the sport at age twenty-three. A journalism major from the University of Maryland, she left the desk-bound life for the

sea in 1986 and threw herself into learning as much about sailboats as possible. A veteran of dozens of long-distance ocean races and years of captaining and crewing on charter vessels, she arrived at the A³ compound with a comprehensive knowledge of boat maintenance and a Coast Guard captain's license certifying her to operate vessels up to one hundred tons.

Klybert, who was soon nicknamed "Dianimal" for the energy with which she threw her six-foot body into everything she did, almost inadvertently passed up the chance to join the team. Working on a boat in the Caribbean, Diana was handed a message one

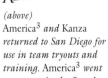

(above)
America³ and Kanza returned to San Diego for use in team tryouts and training. America³ went on to race in the first three rounds of the defender trials.

(left)
Among the first of the women to arrive in San Diego, Diana Klybert helped prepare the compound and boats for the tryout sessions and then was selected as a team member.

15

Melissa Purdy (right), a two-time All-American Woman Sailor and graduate of Brown University, learned to sail on the challenging waters of San Francisco Bay where she and her J-24 Small Flying Patio Furniture made a name for themselves.

(left page) New Englander Lisa Charles brought a RYA Yachtmasters offshore license and a good deal of big-boat experience to the team.

day by her captain. "Know anyone named Kimo? He called and wants you to call him back." The name wasn't immediately identifiable to her and the message was filed away with no response. Several days later, Klybert came across the name in a sailing magazine, identifying Kimo as part of the victorious America's Cup team. She found the message and raced to a phone, followed by her curious skipper. When she got Worthington on the line and heard what he had to say, she wrote in big letters on a piece of paper for her now-former captain to read: AMERICA'S CUP!

Not many women can boast of possessing an RYA Yachtmasters offshore license, the U.K. equivalent to a U.S. Coast Guard license, but Lisa Charles earned hers in 1993. Although she had only taken up sailing three years earlier, she had done so on a full-time basis, racing big boats in Europe and the Caribbean, working transatlantic voyages on the elegant J-Class yacht *Endeavour*, and captaining a forty-footer in Maine. She also worked for famed fashion designer Donna Karan in New York, where she suggested nautical themes for several creations. When her application was received, detailing her experience with big boats and competency with maintaining them, she was asked to help in the early preparations.

A native of Tiburon, California, Melissa Purdy learned to sail and race in the challenging waters of San Francisco Bay. Few who

Many hands make light work as thousands of square feet of sail fabric is pulled aboard after rounding a leeward mark.

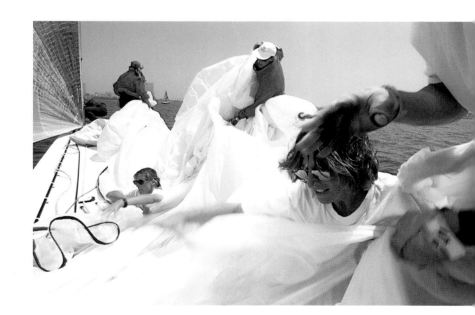

Tryouts for the team in April and May of 1994 gave the opportunity to women throughout the United States to prove themselves in on-the-water action.

raced against her forgot either her competitiveness or the name of the J-24 she steered around the buoys: *Small Flying Patio Furniture*. She took her skills to the highly regarded women's sailing team at Brown University and was named an All-American Woman Sailor in 1990 and 1991. Following graduation, she worked in several jobs before returning to international sailboat racing, mostly in Australia. A competitor thought highly enough of her to recommend to America[3] that she be hired to help set up the compound and the boats for the tryouts.

While the core team introduced in New York was the result of a selection process based on the known abilities and accomplishments of the nine women, the team that would eventually race on the waters off Point Loma, San Diego, was the result of a nationwide search. More than 650 applicants flooded the 1-800-WOMEN-A3 phone line in just three weeks, looking for a chance to be invited to the tryouts. The qualifying sessions were noted for the world-class athletes who arrived at the North Harbor Drive compound prepared to prove themselves in the exercise room, on the water in seventy-five-foot racing machines, and in strategy meetings. Not all were sailors. The coaching staff considered rowers, weight

lifters, bodybuilders, track-and-field specialists, even a ballet dancer. Some of the women walked on a sailboat for the first time when they boarded *America[3]* and *Kanza*. Others battled seasickness. A few, very few, decided almost immediately this wasn't for them. All the others decided it was one of the most exciting times of their lives.

The tryouts were rigorous, giving the hopefuls a taste of what would become a daily routine for the next year should they make the team. Wake-up calls rang before the sun rose, and the day began with a strenuous physical workout in the compound's gym, filled with all types of strength-enhancing and conditioning machines.

The tryouts also demonstrated that part of winning yacht races occurs off-the-water. Maintenance, sail packing, and chalk talks were all part of the routine.

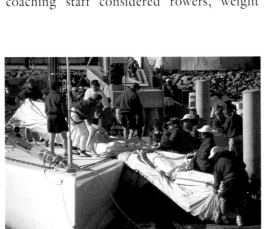

It was in the gym that the women first became acquainted with Dick Dent, former trainer for the San Diego Padres, and the man who was mostly responsible for building the strength of the 1992 A^3 men's team. Dent's knowledge of human physiology and his professional approach to helping the women condition themselves and build their strength was a key to the success they had.

After a brisk jog and a carbo-loaded breakfast next door at Tarantino's Restaurant, the candidates prepared the boats for four to six hours on the water.

While at sea, the coaches rotated the women at different positions, grading them as they tacked and jibed, climbed the mast, hoisted and doused the spinnaker, steered and called tactics. Even for the women who came on board with years of sailing experience, operating an IACC boat with only women performing the jobs was a new undertaking. Exhilarating to some, exhausting to most, the

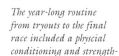

The year-long routine from tryouts to the final race included a physcial conditioning and strength-enhancing program.

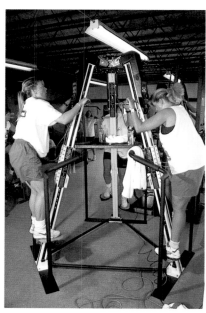

Tarantino's Restaurant was the official supplier of high-energy breakfasts for the women's team.

tryouts gave the A^3 management an opportunity to see how the women worked with each other, how much effort they put into their tasks, and what type of attitude they showed up with each morning.

Certainly, talent was important, but the women quickly learned that Koch's oft-stated criteria of teamwork and attitude counted for more than a mantel filled with trophies. A year in the tight quarters of a boat, performing under the stress of competition, can turn into a nightmare if the right balance of self-reliance and dependency is missing. A quote from George Bernard Shaw, posted on the team bulletin board, seemed to sum up the America^3 message: "The reasonable man adapts himself to conditions that surround him. The unreasonable man adapts his surroundings to himself. All progress depends on one unreasonable man."

The coaches were surprised by how quickly most of the women adapted themselves to their surroundings. Wally Henry, one of five 1992 A^3 men who coached through the tryouts, was quoted in the *New York Times* as saying: "We've covered about one-half the

maneuvers they're going to have to learn. We never thought we'd be so far along so soon."

What came out of the tryouts, aside from twenty-two women who made up the America^3 sailing team, was that the women were extremely coachable. It was said they were more willing to follow advice than their male counterparts of the previous campaign and that they came together as a team much quicker.

"We have been overwhelmed by the quality of the women at these tryouts," Koch

Captain of conditioning, Dick Dent put the women through their paces in the gym as he had done with the men's team in 1992.

told the media. "They have fire in their bellies, they have a killer instinct, they really want to win. You're going to see them change sailing forever."

Selecting the final team from the candidates who came to San Diego was not an easy task. Talent was in abundance. The women handled the boat well. Strength did not appear to be an issue. But sailing around for a week and racing competitively for months on end were two very different situations. In addition to assessing how each individual would fit within a team, those doing the selecting considered personality, motivation, and capacity to perform under pressure. As Stu Argo, Worthington's assistant, said: "We had to figure out who was able to go the distance and work with the team for the entire year."

Worthington, Argo, and the coaches who worked the tryouts gave their input to Koch and Moeyersoms. Towards the end of May, after many discussions and more than a few moments of soul-searching, the first all-women's team in the 143-year history of the America's Cup was selected. Those who made

the team were given one week to decide if they truly were able to make the commitment.

Within the world of competitive sailing, there was probably more immediate talk about who didn't make the team than about who did. Some of the best-known names in women's sailing were not asked back. The coaches and management at America³ steadfastly refused to elaborate on why they did or didn't make specific choices. The chief criteria of teamwork and attitude had long been established and explained. Some decisions may have resulted from simple observations as the one recalled by a coach after one of the tryout sessions: "When, after a long, hard day on the water you notice one of the candidates sitting in a chair eating a sandwich and drinking a soda while every other person is working at putting the boat and sails away, 'team player' are not the first two words that come to mind."

And while talent was evident, some of the women with a great deal of sailing experience had gained it in dinghies racing solo or with one crew. Some found it difficult to transfer their small-boat skills to a seventy-five-foot

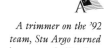

A trimmer on the '92 team, Stu Argo turned down several offers from other syndicates in favor of helping to coach the women's team.

IACC yacht which requires sixteen sailors working as a coordinated team to operate it at full potential. And a few others determined that the disruption to home, work, and family was too great a price to pay for the opportunity extended to them.

On June 1, 1994, six months before the first round of races in the defender elimination trials was to begin, twenty-two women making up America[3]—The Women's Team reported to work at 4960 North Harbor Drive in San Diego. Six more women joined the team at various times during those six months.

Actually, there were twenty-three women who had originally been selected, counting Alison Townley, who, as a member of the core team presented at the New York announcement, had expected to be able to compete before a back injury forced her to the sidelines. But Townley's skills went beyond those she

used to become an Olympic rower and win twenty-two U.S. rowing titles. Personable and articulate, her potential contributions to the overall effort off the water were recognized by A[3] management, and she became the team's official spokeswoman and goodwill ambassador. Her job took her throughout the United States, one day explaining the team to a Girl Scout group, the next facing a boardroom full of pinstripe executives. As well, Townley represented America[3] during a twenty-city tour put together by three of the syndicate's sponsors—Motorola, Gillette, and *Glamour* magazine.

Each of the four women—Klybert, Charles, Oetking, and Purdy—who helped prepare the compound and the boats for the tryouts made the team, but Oetking later chose to leave. Doubly effective at sea and on land, they served as examples for demonstrating

that a sailing team's success is the result of more than just its performance on the water. During the year the team was together, every member became proficient in maintenance duties, whether it be cleaning and lubricating winch gears or repairing torn sails. For those women who would continue sailing careers, their value to future teams was perhaps more greatly enhanced by what they learned or refined ashore as it was by honing their racing skills.

Although no positions on board had been assigned, it was fairly evident whose abilities were more appropriate for the strength positions and who was best qualified for sail handling or trimming or the afterguard. From the very beginning, athletes whose achievements had been noted in the sport of rowing were encouraged to try out for the team. Aside from their obvious pure strength, what made them attractive as potential grinders was their endurance, cardiovascular development, and ability to explode in short bursts of energy, all ideal qualities in supplying the power needed to trim the sails.

Amy Baltzell, Sarah Bergeron, Amy Fuller, Stephanie Maxwell-Pierson, Marci Porter, and Anna Seaton-Huntington all had extensive rowing experience ranging from top-ranked collegiate crews to the U.S. Olympic Rowing Team.

Baltzell made the 1992 Olympic Rowing Team after capturing the gold medal in the 1991 women's eight competition in Lucerne, Switzerland. A dedicated athlete since early in her youth, she was recruited by Wesleyan University to bring her five-foot, eleven-inch height to the women's basketball team. She also joined the crew team, and after her fresh-

man year, she chose to concentrate on rowing. Her performance in that sport earned her numerous medals and added to her appreciation of teamwork, an attitude that immediately impressed Worthington. "Within the first couple of days," said the director of sailing operations about Baltzell's tryout, "we knew Amy was just right for the team. Her height, strength, and, most of all, her attitude, all fit perfectly."

Growing up in Middletown, New Jersey, Sarah Bergeron competed in field hockey, swimming, soccer, basketball, and rowing. Her

(left page)
A former basketball player and member of the 1992 Olympic rowing team, Amy Baltzell brought her strength and athletic ability to the team and secured a position as grinder.

(below)
New Jersey native Sarah Bergeron was a veteran of field hockey, swimming, soccer, basketball, and rowing competitions. She ranked first among collegiates in a national strength test.

ranked her first among all collegiate rowers and fourth in the U.S. At age twenty-two, she shared the title "youngest team member" on America³ with Katie Pettibone.

One of the women to join the team after the first selection was made, Amy Fuller had a silver medal in rowing from the 1992 Olympics and was training for the '96 Games when she was asked to join America³. With twenty-six national and international titles in rowing, she was somewhat reluctant to leave the sport she knew so well and had excelled at for so long to enter a sport she knew nothing about. But in the midst of her fifth year on the U.S. National Rowing Team and after being named in 1993 as the U.S. Rowing Female of the Year, Fuller was given the go-ahead by her coach. She moved to San Diego in November,

prowess in rowing earned her a scholarship to George Washington University, where she received a varsity letter in each of her four years there. In her final two and a half years she was judged the strongest rower on the college team. Her ERG score, a national test for strength, endurance, and mental toughness,

adding more strength and power to the demanding position of grinder. Like most of the women on the team, she recognized the impact the effort would have on sailing in general and the America's Cup in particular. "Sailing is a very male, very rich sport," she told a reporter. "The reason women don't have experience in the America's Cup is because we've been discriminated against. That's what we're changing, hopefully."

When Stephanie Maxwell-Pierson and Anna Seaton Huntington teamed up to win the Olympic bronze medal in the women's pair rowing competition in Barcelona, there's little doubt either ever thought they would be sailing in the America's Cup trials in three years. Maxwell-Pierson had always been prone to seasickness and had little desire to spend much time on any boat other than a scull. Seaton Huntington was more interested in completing a journalism degree at Columbia University than in taking up a new sport. But when she returned home one night in September 1993 to hear Bill Koch's voice on her answering machine asking if she might be interested in discussing the possibility of a women's America's Cup team, the Kansas native returned the call that led to both her and Maxwell-Pierson's joining the core team.

The athletic career of Maxwell-Pierson stretched over eleven years and had garnered her eighteen international and sixteen national titles. Named the Female Athlete of the Year by the U.S. Rowing Association in 1990 (with Seaton Huntington) and 1991, she was a star on the crew team at Cornell University where she was later inducted into their athletic hall of fame. When she first heard of America[3]—in a phone call from Koch—she had retired from

athletics and was pursuing a business career in hotel management. But the attraction of a new sporting challenge proved too great, and after convincing her husband, Greg, to postpone his career plans for a year, the two moved to San Diego.

After the initial announcement in New York, Seaton Huntington returned to Columbia to complete her journalism degree. The plan had been for her to join the women's team after her studies were completed, but a wedding came first. She had met Stewart Huntington, a reporter with the *San Francisco Examiner*, when she competed in the 1988 Olympics in Seoul, Korea. A romance began, then was interrupted by time and distance, but was rekindled several years later, and the couple took the opportunity to wed in October 1994, well after the women's team had formed. The offer to try out for the team remained alive, and in late November she arrived in San Diego.

When a knee injury in 1988 ended Marci Porter's basketball career at the University of

The other part of the Olympic bronze medal performance with Maxwell-Pierson, Anna Seaton Huntington (on right) graduated from Harvard and was attending Columbia Journalism School when she received a phone call from fellow Kansan Bill Koch.

California at Davis, she simply took her athletic skills to the crew team where she quickly rose to championship status. As a member of the national rowing team from 1991 to 1993, she was an alternate for the 1992 Olympic team and was in training for the 1996 Olympics when she joined America[3]. Among her rowing credits was a first in the 1993 U.S. national women's pair; first in women's eight, four, and pairs in the 1992 U.S. National Championships; first in the 1989 and 1990 Olympic Festival women's eight and four; and first in the senior women's eight at the 1990

Royal Canadian Henley. Porter was one of the more enthusiastic team members, entering into both the athletic and social life with exuberance. And while she took to her new sport with dedication, she continued training for what she hoped would be a rowing seat in the 1996 Olympics by working out in her single scull whenever possible.

Stephanie Armitage-Johnson was not a rower, but was selected for the team based on her strength accomplishments. She is a world-class weight lifter with a master's degree in exercise science. When Armitage-Johnson learned about the team from her husband Fred, she was working as an assistant strength and conditioning coach for the University of Washington football team, one of only four women in the nation to hold such a position. As a weight lifter, she had become one of the top five women in the super-heavy and heavy-weight divisions between 1989 and 1993. She

had won gold and silver medals in the Olympic Sports Festival and had long been a proponent of encouraging girls and women into male-dominated sports. Her position with A³ was an extension of her desire to reduce, if not eliminate, gender bias in athletics.

The women who were invited to try out because of their sailing credentials had a wide variety of experience in cruising and racing, from short courses to long distance. Some had competed in club competitions, others were Olympic veterans. One of the core team, Dawn Riley, had yet to arrive in San Diego to try out. However, her excuse for the long absence was quite acceptable—she'd been skippering the boat *Heineken* in the 1993-94 Whitbread 'Round-the-World race. Her skills were well known to America³, as she was the only

woman on the 1992 team. At the conclusion of the Whitbread, she had two offers: a position on the PACT '95 team or an opportunity to try out for the America³ team. She chose the tryout. Riley made the women's team and was selected as crew boss and team captain.

Working the foredeck on *Heineken* was Merritt Carey, who was encouraged to apply for the A³ team by an impressed Skipper Riley. From Tenants Harbor, Maine, she had sailed all her life, including transatlantic and Fastnet races. Like Purdy and another teammate, Hannah Swett, Carey attended Brown University. After graduation, she began a journalism career, but, also like many of her teammates, sailing proved to be a stronger calling and she left a desk behind for time at sea.

Dawn Riley became captain of the women's team, a position well suited to her experience, which included two Whitbread races and the 1992 America's Cup defender trials with America³.

Swett, also a New Englander from Jamestown, Rhode Island, began sailing when she was ten and first demonstrated her racing prowess on a national level in 1984 when she placed first in the 420 class at the High School Nationals. At Brown, she roomed with Purdy and was named an All-American Woman Sailor in 1989 and 1991. She won the Collegiate Nationals in 1989 and then went on to win many U.S. and international titles, including: first in the 1991 Fastnet; first in the J-24 class at the 1993 Rolex Regatta; first in the 1993 Lightning Atlantic Coast; and first in the 1993 Women's Lightning Championships. As a sailing coach in Newport, Rhode Island, she was skeptical of rumors she had heard about the team—she knew the game well and in the past there had never been money for a women's America's Cup team. But when the announcement turned the rumors to reality, she quickly applied.

Two Olympic sailors made the team. Leslie Egnot and JJ Isler both competed in the 1992 Olympics in Barcelona, Spain, in the

Hannah Swett was an accomplished collegiate sailor at Brown and brought many titles with her to the America[3] sailing team. She was on board as a trimmer for every race in the 1995 campaign.

(left page)
A shipmate of Riley's aboard Heineken in the 1993-94 Whitbread, Merritt Carey viewed the sailing world from a number of perspectives.

women's 470 class. Egnot won a silver medal and Isler took the bronze. Although born in South Carolina, Egnot moved with her family to New Zealand in 1973, and it was there that she learned to sail and later became recognized as one of the country's top racing sailors. Beginning in 1985 and continuing every year until she joined America[3], Egnot won the New Zealand Women's 470 championship. Among other titles, she was also the New Zealand Women's Keelboat champion in 1990, 1991, and 1993. Dawn Riley had raced with her in New Zealand and encouraged her to apply for

Silver medalist in the 470 class during the '92 Barcelona Olympics, Leslie Egnot became helmsman of the women's team in Cup racing.

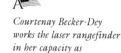

1986 and 1991. In addition to being the first to cross the finish line in countless races, she was the first woman to skipper a team on the International Match Racing and Formula One circuits. She was also the first woman to be named captain of the Yale varsity sailing team. Isler's family has been involved in the sport for years. Her father, Tom Fetter, was a former commodore of the San Diego Yacht Club. Her husband, Peter, sailed with Dennis Conner in the 1987 and 1988 America's Cups and then joined ESPN as a sailing commentator for the '92 and '95 events. Their daughter, Marly, was born just five months before the new team was announced.

the women's team after she discovered that Egnot held a U.S. passport.

Isler is one of the best-known sailors in the United States. Aside from her Olympic involvement, the racing career she began at age eight has brought her numerous championships and national acclaim, including being named the Rolex Yachtswoman of the Year in

From 1989 to 1994, Courtenay Becker-Dey was ranked number one on the U.S. Sailing Team. She was number five in the world from 1990 through 1993. It was not a

It was that type of foresight and dedication that impressed the America[3] coaching staff, as did her background as an aerospace engineer, consulting to NASA's Microgravity Division. Her husband Bruce was a sales manager for North Sails in Annapolis, Maryland, and the two had cruised and raced on the Chesapeake for years before moving to San Diego, where they lived on a boat during the year the team was together. Leech Nairn won the bow position and was quickly nicknamed "Susie Bow Chick," a sobriquet the media latched onto and repeated with great frequency in newspaper, magazine, and television coverage. It was just one indication that the team found as much humor as seriousness in the much discussed implications of the role of the all-women's team in the America's Cup.

Linda Lindquist was no stranger to the business side of the sport. As marketing director of INTERLUX Yacht Finishes and a principal in helping to establish "Sail Expo," she worked within the industry on a daily basis.

great surprise to her Rye, New York, family that the only girl of four children would devote herself to sailing. A three-week cruise on the family boat before she was three months old was her initiation into the sport, and she began racing when she was eight years old. At a summer camp at age ten, she was coached by Dave Dellenbaugh. Her titles include: Rolex Yachtswoman of the Year; U.S. Olympic Committee's Athlete of the Year in yachting; Gold Medal in the 1990 Pre-Olympics in Barcelona; second and fourth places in the European Dinghy World Championships.

When Susie Leech Nairn first heard about the all-women's team, she made two telephone calls. One was to the 1-800-WOMEN-A3 number and the other was to ESPN, requesting tapes of the 1992 America's Cup. At five feet, three inches, she was well suited to the position of bowman, and with more than seventeen years of experience in competitive sailing, she knew the position well. But she had never competed at the America's Cup level, and she wanted to study the tapes in case there were techniques and particular moves that would help her win a place on the team.

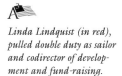

Many of her customers and colleagues were men and women she had sailed with or against during twenty-three years of racing sailboats. The mixture of racing and business suited her well in her new role (make that roles) on the America[3] team. One of the nine women on the core team, Lindquist also signed on as codirector of development and fund-raising. Working two jobs at once was not new to the sailor/businesswoman, as she had funded her college education at the University of Illinois by punching in to several different time clocks throughout the day. Nor was being a member of a women's team new to her—she was a member of the first female crew to compete in the Newport-Bermuda race in 1992.

Lindquist began her days very early on the West Coast in order to reach East Coast corporate executives before she began sailing. And even on the tow out to the race course, the indefatigable marketer could be seen with a cellular phone held to her ear and overheard explaining why the women's team made great promotional sense for whatever company was on the other end of the call.

Indefatigable might also be the most appropriate description of Susan Hemond-Dent, an accomplished endurance athlete who was a member of Team American Pride, the first U.S. team to participate in and complete the Raid Gauloises competition. This incredibly strenuous five-hundred-mile "race" across desert, mountain, and sea in all types of conditions and against all kinds of obstacles taxes the very limits of human fitness. Hemond-Dent, a native of Milwaukee who grew up in San Marino, California, could be said to have been in training for such a survival marathon all her life. As an avid ocean kayaker, rock climber, mountain climber, snow and water skier, certified sky diver, and even camel rider, she was accustomed to physical activity. She was also familiar with America[3]. During the

1992 campaign, she had worked as a sail-team volunteer, and after her application for the women's team was rejected, she once again volunteered to help out whenever and wherever she was needed. Whether she was painting the locker room or climbing a mast, Hemond-Dent made herself indispensable to the effort, and her hard work and positive attitude earned her a place on the team in October. For the past fourteen years, she has worked in television sports production. Dick Dent, the former San Diego Padres trainer and fitness coach of both the 1992 and 1995 America[3] teams, is her husband.

Also joining late was Debbie Pettibone, who had tried out for the team with her sister Katie. At that time there had not been enough room to accommodate both sisters. Katie made

the team, and Debbie returned to Miami. But when it became apparent that more sailors were needed, Debbie was called in August and began with the team in September. Although she grew up in a sailing family in Port Huron, Michigan, Pettibone hated being on board as a young girl. But in her teenage years, she began racing with her father and developed an affection for the sport. Although she raced during the summers, race days at the University of Michigan conflicted with her involvement in the marching band, in which she played clarinet for four years. Still, she found time to crew in numerous races on the Great Lakes and on the Southern Circuit.

The Pettibone sisters found crew positions on racing boats for each other when they were teenagers, and it is somewhat ironic—and

Although the youngest member of the team, Katie Pettibone's sailing experience and abilities earned her a regular spot as trimmer aboard the racing boat.

perhaps fitting—that they both ended up as trimmers, Debbie on port and Katie on starboard. Katie, too, was not enamored of sailing in her youth until she began racing, but she had always been athletic. She broke her high school girls' shot-put record and also threw the discus and played soccer. Eventually, she put her energy into sailing and crewed in races in the midwest and on the SORC in boats ranging from nineteen to fifty feet. When she received a call from Worthington about the new team, she was working toward a degree in marine biology at the University of Miami. As both a sailor and a certified diver, she had spent a good deal of time on and under the surface of the seas and had determined that she wanted to make a career of working with sea mammals. To that end, she had founded the Marine Mammal Stranding Network with the aid of the university's marine biology department and that of the National Marine Fisheries Service.

Detroit native Merritt Palm was a product of junior sailing programs and Miami University of Ohio's sailing team, which she captained for two years.

Katie rotated as starboard trimmer with Merritt Palm, a Detroit native who also had grown up in a sailing family. She spent summers cruising and gained racing experience in junior programs. As her proficiency in small boats grew, she became increasingly successful at racing and was ranked among the top ten U.S. sailors in the European dinghy. Palm was the captain of the Miami University of Ohio's sailing team for two years and, after graduating in 1990 with a degree in English and political science, she worked as a sailing instructor and substitute elementary school teacher. Her brother Justin, a friend of Stu Argo, first heard about the women's team from Argo and suggested that his sister apply. Wary of big boats, as she was training for an Olympic campaign, she initially resisted. But with continued encouragement from Justin, she finally did apply and was invited to the third tryout, where she proved herself. Through the months of training, she carefully studied Argo, a trimmer during the 1992 campaign, and realized that big-boat technique was different. She built on her small-boat skills and developed big-boat expertise quickly.

Few, if any, women sailors in the United States have won more medals than Annie Nelson. After beginning the sport at age nine, she got her first Sunfish at twelve and began racing with her father that very year. Since then, she has collected more than fifty championships and fifteen national and international titles. Long before America³ organized its team, Nelson had assembled her own women's crew to race with her in the 1981 and 1982 SORC regattas. She was a member of the U.S. Women's World Sailing Team in 1982, 1983, and 1994, and was named Yachtswoman of the

Year by three different organizations in 1983. Along the way, she also took up board sailing, at which she also excelled, and won a silver medal in the 1984 Olympic Board Sailing Exhibition. And with famed sixty-five-year-old daredevil windsurfer Jack Wood, she crossed Lake Titicaca in Peru, the world's highest navigable lake, on a sailboard in 1981. Her husband Bruce was a designer for rival cup contender PACT '95, establishing them as the first married couple to be involved with opposing America's Cup teams.

One of Nelson's teammates in the 1981 SORC was Sarah Cavanagh, who had grown up sailing in New England since the age of three. She, too, was used to women's teams,

Few, if any, women in the U.S. have won more medals than Annie Nelson. She was one of three mothers on the team.

(below)
Sarah Cavanagh was a veteran of a number of all-women's teams and had been a crew member in several long-distance ocean races.

A sailor since early childhood, Christy Evans also played varsity soccer and ice hockey at Bowdoin College.

(right page) While attending the U.S. Coast Guard Academy, Joan Touchette was captain of the women's sailing team. She worked the mast for America³.

having competed on them in the Rolex International Regatta, the Fort Lauderdale to Jamaica race, and the La Rochelle (France) to New Orleans race. Besides racing, she had worked in several other capacities involving different types of boats: a deckhand on three-masted schooners; repairing sails; managing a sailing school and dive boat concern; and running a boatyard. Cavanagh had also earned a degree in yacht design from the Landing School in Kennebunkport, Maine. One of only three mothers (with Isler and Nelson) on the team, her seven-year-old son, Matthew, lived with his father in Massachusetts during the campaign.

Another New Englander, Christy Evans, learned to sail when her parents enrolled her in a Marblehead, Massachusetts, town program. She continued through several summers at Girl Scout camp and began racing early in life. Other sports were also an attraction, and at Bowdoin College, she was a member of the varsity soccer and ice hockey teams. As tacti-

cian and sail trimmer, Evens competed in the 1989 and 1991 U.S. Rolex International Women's Keelboat Championships. After graduation in 1985, she worked in a variety of jobs, including production manager at Doyle Sailmakers' spinnaker loft. She was encouraged to apply to America³ by Bobby Campbell, a member of the 1992 team. At first reluctant to do so because of her job in Boston and the belief that she didn't have a chance, she finally did and was invited to the final tryout. After returning to Boston, she told her boss she wouldn't make the team, but had to disabuse him of that notion after Worthington called and asked her if she'd like to live in San Diego for a year.

A native of Columbia, Maryland, Joan Touchette spent a good deal of her youth cruising and racing on Chesapeake Bay. With supportive parents who used to drive their daughter and her Laser to regattas up and down the East Coast, Touchette honed her skills and acquired a room full of medals. Her

Sponsors' logos were well displayed throughout the campaign.

(left)
Cover model Christie
Brinkley hosted a Lifetime
cable network program on
the women's team called
"Rocking the Boat."

Citizen Watch, Dry Idea from Gillette, *Glamour* magazine, H$_2$O Plus, Hewlett-Packard, Lifetime Television, and Motorola. The contributing suppliers were BOAT/U.S., Columbia Sportswear, Domaine Chandon, Hyatt Regency San Diego, and Saucony.

While the extraordinary nature of the team merely attracted contributors and spon-

sors, it drew the international press like sharks to blood. Even before the March announcement, San Diego and New York newspapers published articles speculating about Koch's plans. Once those plans were made public, it seemed that everyone carrying a press card, pen, or microphone was requesting access to the women. Trying to bring some sense of order to it all was Will Robinson, who, as director of communications and public relations, no doubt often felt he was driving a runaway train. More than twenty-five thousand media requests flooded the compound switchboard. Everyone from network anchorpeople to high school newspaper reporters wanted a shot at the breaking story. Robinson is a savvy newsman with experience in both broadcast media and America's Cup campaigns. He took over as media director of the 1992 America[3]

Bill Koch shakes hands with
Hewlett-Packard executive
Clark Straw as Richard
Schwartz (to left of Koch)
of Boat U.S. and
Chevrolet's Steve McAvoy
look on.

effort in time to handle the onslaught that led to and followed the victory. Formerly a managing editor at KCBS-TV News in Los Angeles and special projects producer at KRON-TV in San Francisco, Robinson spent a good deal of time at the beginning of the 1995 campaign organizing media training sessions for the women.

Even for the more seasoned athletes who had competed in the Olympic Games, the intensity and longevity of the spotlight was new. For some it was fun, others found it disconcerting, and many came to view the

attention as an intrusion and the repetitive questions as maddening. But the significance of the overwhelming coverage was lost on no one. Each of the team members knew that publicity was the key to attracting sponsors. And if the message of equality in the sport was one of the goals of the campaign, everyone was cognizant of the fact that it was through the media that that message was most efficiently and effectively communicated.

As associate director of communications and public relations, Sandra Bateman assisted Robinson and the women through the chaos. With a background in advertising and public relations at Apple Computer, Magnavox, Motorola, and Trimble Navigation, she brought a clear understanding of the importance of technology in sailing, especially as it applies to the America's Cup.

While Robinson and Bateman worked with the electronic and print media, photographic and video images from inside the compound and aboard the boats were produced and distributed by Daniel Forster and Phil Uhl. Both men had held similar positions with the 1992 campaign and had years of experience in the marine field.

As director of public affairs, Pamela Julias brought some twenty years of experience in public and government affairs to the job. She began working in the campaign as a consultant from Howard J. Rubenstein Associates in New York City before Bill Koch hired her for a split position with America[3] and his Oxbow Corporation.

While there was a hint of the interest the women's team would create as far back as the September 1994 Cape Cod meeting when Robinson held his first media training session,

no one anticipated the avalanche of coverage that resulted. From the time of the March announcement until well after the last race, there was not a day that went by that some publication or newscast, somewhere on earth, did not run a piece about the team. Clipping services provided copies of articles and radio and television transcripts that, when stacked on top of each other, formed a tower of newsprint more than five feet tall. When it was all over, almost three billion impressions on the team were recorded. To buy the same amount of print space and television time would have cost close to $50 million. There was no question that the women's team was the subject of more stories than all of the other 1995 America's Cup teams combined, and it was estimated that it also generated more press interest than

all of the America's Cups through history. It's fair to say it was a media phenomenon unlikely to ever be duplicated.

Immediately after the New York announcement, the initial press and public reaction was mostly positive, although there were those in both sectors who decried the women's lack of experience and strength. Some of the Old Guard, blue-blazered Corinthians resisted the concept, uncomfortable that one of the last bastions of male dominance was going the way of men-only clubs and segregated schools. But by the time the team was chosen with its roster of irrefutable world-class sailors and athletes, the strength issue had long been dismissed and only the question of experience, the stated reason for establishing the team, remained.

The team poses in front of their logo-decorated keel on April 9,1995 during "Reveal Your Keel Day," when all syndicates still competing were obligated to show the undersides of their yachts.

THE BOATS

Match racing, in which two boats race against each other, is the format used in the America's Cup. While this particular style of racing has its own set of tactics and strategies and is generally believed to result in the better sailors emerging victorious, the America's Cup tends to place more of an emphasis on boat development than on sailing skills. That's not to say that sailors are secondary to the effort—the mere fact that the best sailors in the world are selected to race in the Cup is proof of that—but it is to point out that new technologies have been the focus of this regatta throughout history.

In many respects, it could be said that the America^3 boat designed and built for the 1995 Cup races began a decade before. It was then that Bill Koch teamed up with Dr. Jerry Milgram, naval architect and professor of ocean engineering at the Massachusetts Institute of Technology, to initiate two research programs that have had profound effects on modern America's Cup boat design. One was theoretical and resulted in significant advances in the Velocity Prediction Program (VPP), a relatively new, evolving formula meant to predict a particular boat's speed under given conditions with certain sails hoisted. The other program was aimed at designing the fastest maxi-boat in existence. That was accomplished with the development of *Matador^2*, Koch's famous racer that won two world titles and set a standard still unmatched today. The yacht was the result of Koch's scientific approach to sailboat racing. He is a proponent of the creative process, pushing his people for as many ideas as they can devise. The process is then tempered by a system of checks and balances derived from exhaustive testing. Koch describes the process as "science making the decisions while intuition comes up with ideas. There is no magic involved. Fundamental scientific principles are the way to go. The person who wins a boat race is the most objective."

Through this process, a whole new set of design tools have evolved over the decade, perhaps Koch's greatest contribution to naval architecture. In addition, great advances were made in the fields of composite research, engineering, computer modeling, full-scale testing, tactical software, sail making, and construction.

Koch's plan for the 1992 Cup was to design and build four new boats, the third of which, *America^3*, was the 4-1 victor in the actual Cup match with Italy. That boat was used by the women's team during the tryouts, in the IACC World Championships, and through the first three rounds of the

1995 Cup. The final '92 boat produced, *Kanza*, was used as the tuning and training boat during the 1995 campaign.

The success of the '92 team and boats surprised most Cup competitors and observers and gained worldwide respect for the Koch team. Even those who denigrated the women's team idea grudgingly admitted that the boats and technology available to them, plus the new work of design and construction teams, would probably place the women on at least an equal footing with the men's teams.

Koch had promised a new boat if sponsorship in early '95 was sufficient enough to support production. Because so much research and development had already been done both in the *Matador* project and in the building of the four '92 boats, neither as much money nor testing was necessary. However, that did not mean that America[3] could rest on its laurels. While it was true that the boat that won in the previous Cup was ahead of its time, every syndicate coming to San Diego was undoubtedly modeling their new boats on *America*[3]. The

The exhaustive research and development program included tank testing, model building, and advanced construction methods.

An IACC model being
prepared for tank testing.
Everything from keel shapes
and rudder lengths were
tested in an exhaustive
research program that led to
the design of Mighty Mary.

The construction of Mighty
Mary was undertaken
at Eric Goetz Custom
Sailboats in Bristol, Rhode
Island. Goetz expertise was
highly valued - the company
built all of the American
Cup boats.

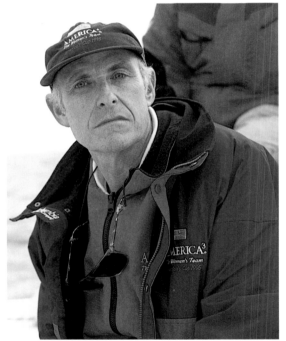

boat had set the standard and now everyone knew that the 1995 winner would have to beat that standard by significant margins.

Charged with doing just that within the A^3 syndicate was the technology and design team led by Peter Wilson, Dr. Heiner Meldner, Dr. Jerry Milgram, and Dr. William Unkel, all veterans of the '92 effort. As director of the team, Wilson was responsible for the overall implementation of the design, construction, and engineering plans. Meldner, a physicist, software developer, designer, and inventor had been involved in America's Cup campaigns

since 1977. His particular area of expertise was the development of appendages. Unkel's field of expertise is in creating software, particularly for instrument and electronic systems. His experience with both the *Matador* and '92 programs was a boon to the new team.

To produce the new boat, the designers had to work within the IACC rule, part of which states that the aim of the design para-meters is to produce "wholesome day-sailing monohulls of similar performance while foster-ing design developments that will flow through the mainstream of yachting." That was the ideal. The practical application of it was well said by Jim Taylor, a designer who played important roles in both the '92 and '95 A^3 campaigns. Writing in the syndicate's newsletter, he ventured: "While some may question how 'wholesome' or 'mainstream' some of the forty-three IACC yachts built under the rule have turned out to be, there is no question that this rule has fostered an explosion of design development and technical ingenuity. The A^3 design team has always believed one of the keys to success for the Women's Team is that we leapfrog USA-23 (*America^3*) further than anyone else in the design of our new boat."

That was the challenge, the same as that which faced every other syndicate. But America^3 had the advantage of knowing the exact design of USA-23, and they had been trying to "leapfrog" it since 1992. As Koch said, "Last time we had the optimum boat. It will not be the optimum boat for this Cup because everybody will be trying to copy it or improve on it. Trying to improve on *America^3* didn't take us anywhere in '92. It only made us slower. So the new boat is going to have to be radically different."

Koch's point was that he estimated it cost $40 million to achieve a speed of 9.235 knots and another $30 million to increase it to 9.3 knots. He feels $25 million was spent "going down blind alleys." But it was $25 million that didn't have to be spent again in quest of the radically different boat that would outperform not only *America^3*, but all the other new creations.

The construction team at Goetz Custom Sailboats pose next to their work for the America^3 women's team.

The team's first real competition occured at the end of July, 1994 in Newport, Rhode Island after just six weeks of training together as a team.

THE RACES

The promise of the women's team made itself evident in two 1994 regattas before America's Cup racing began. After some six weeks of intense physical and on-water training in San Diego, the team moved east for the New York Yacht Club's Sesquicentennial Regatta in Newport, Rhode Island. Scheduled from July 23 to 30, the event celebrated the founding of the famed yacht club that for 132 years had held the trophy the women's team intended to capture.

The A^3 syndicate had come to Newport in force. The women's team would sail as a complete unit aboard *Matador*^{2}, which required a contingent of men from the 1992 team to fill all the positions. Koch had also leased *Kiwi Magic*, the twelve-meter New Zealand speedster from the 1986-87 Cup trials in Fremantle, Australia. Accommodations were found in houses dotting the waterfront and at Salve Regina College. With 214 boats entered in the regatta and several thousand spectators in town just to be part of the event, Newport was choked with humanity. The trip to Newport was ostensibly a continuation of the training regimen underway in San Diego, but it was also viewed as a timely break, a bit of fun, and a chance to let the sailing establishment have a look at the women's team from a perspective other than down their noses.

The women acquitted themselves well aboard *Matador*^{2} and served notice that they would be serious contenders in California. But it was an off-the-water incident that drew the greatest amount of attention to the team and and may have solidified Dennis Conner's reputation as the most controversial figure in the sport. At a party in honor of the Stars & Stripes team hosted by America^3, Conner drunkenly launched into his now-infamous "bunch of Lesbos" appraisal of the newly-formed Cup competitors. Aiming his comments at longtime friend Annie Nelson, whose husband Bruce had been a key member of past design teams for the skipper, Conner managed to become overwrought and overheated in a matter of minutes. Hoping to douse the fire somewhat, Annie tipped her bottle of mineral water (later erroneously reported to be everything from a plastic cup of rum and coke to a magnum of champagne) over Conner's head, and as its contents dripped onto his extremely surprised countenance, the gauntlet was thrown down. It was a spontaneous gesture, certainly provoked by boorish behavior, and it spoke volumes that this team wasn't going to take any crap from anyone, on or off the water.

A better indication of how the women would perform in competition occurred at the IACC World Championship, held in San Diego between October 27 and November 5. In this event, they were racing for the first time on the same type of boat, the International America's Cup Class, that they

would race in the Cup competition beginning in less than two months. Neither a helmsman nor a "first-string" roster had been selected. Leslie Egnot, JJ Isler, and Dawn Riley would rotate at the wheel, and many combinations in the afterguard, at the strength positions, and the sail handlers and trimmers were tried. The idea was not so much to win every race as to gain as much experience as possible and to see which crew worked best together.

All three American syndicates competed, albeit none with new boats. Only two challengers, oneAustralia and Nippon Challenge, fielded teams for the IACC Worlds, and both syndicates raced new yachts. In their first-ever race against men on America's Cup boats, the America[3] women's team, racing on the 1992 vintage *America[3]*, finished second to the newly built *oneAustralia*. It was a significant achievement, just as crossing the finish line first in the final race was further evidence that this team was not a joke, not a publicity stunt, not the whim of a millionaire. Completing the regatta in second place overall, behind *oneAustralia*, the women proved a point.

Perhaps Mike O'Connor, writing for the *Boston Herald*, said it best:

> *The women's team. The all-female boat. The girls. The chics. The Just Not Good Enoughs. The America[3] crew that competed at the International America's Cup Class World Championships, which wrapped up Saturday, was called everything but the Sea Hens as critics derided its chances against seasoned all-male teams. Perhaps a new name is now in order: sailors. Very good, very competitive ones.*

IACC boats parade under spinnaker in front of downtown San Diego.

(left page)
During the New York Yacht Club's Sesquicentennial Regatta in Newport, RI, the women's team sailed Koch's famous maxi-racer Matador[2].

The goal for the period between the end of the Worlds and the start of the America's Cup was to learn from the few racing experiences the team had had together. Worthington, Argo, and the rest of the coaches prepared lists of what they felt the team needed to work on most, what weaknesses they had seen in Newport, in a short series of October races against a number of the 1992 men's team, and in the Worlds. Dent continued to work on physical conditioning and building strength. Sessions on strategy and tactics started earlier and ended later. On the water, it was two-boat testing, practice starts, simulated races, jibe sets, straight-line take-downs, downspeed tacking duels, sail testing, and mast tuning. All in all, it became obvious that the biggest shortcoming of the aggregate group was the one everyone knew before the first team member was selected—experience. And that was exactly what all of A[3] hoped to remedy in the early rounds of the defender trials.

*The IACC World
Championships in
1994 drew seven entries,
including the women's
team, which finished
second.*

The format of the Citizen Cup, the defender races sponsored by the watch company of the same name, called for four round-robins, followed by a semifinal and final series to determine which of the three American teams would advance to the America's Cup match as the defender. The original schedule called for four round-robins to be sailed between January 12 and March 10, with each of the teams racing each other three times in each round. Since there were just three teams, each would advance to the semifinals with the first-place team after the four rounds carrying forward two points, the second-place team one point, and the third none. Then the two teams with the highest scores would race each other in the finals. That was the way it was originally scheduled, anyway.

As the January 12 date approached, Worthington, Moeyersoms, and the coaches

were faced with some very hard choices. There were sixteen positions on the boat and twenty-eight women on the team. The talent was unquestioned. The work ethic was obvious. The historical significance of the effort was lost on no one, and, of course, everyone wanted to race.

The final selection of each day's lineup rested with Kimo Worthington, who no doubt

John Marshall, Dennis Conner, and Bill Koch all had designs on the Citizen Cup while the watchmaker's president, Larry Gruenstein, looks on.

(below)
Opening ceremonies of the 1995 defender races brought color and pageantry to the event.

(below)
The women receive a rainy send-off for their first official race in round-robin one on January 13, 1995.

found some relief in the fact that as many as five months of racing and the possibility of fifty different lineup selections loomed ahead. That allowed a lot of time for crew rotation. Five grinders were needed every race, but the physical demands of the position necessitated frequent substitutions. Throughout the 1995 Cup season, Marci Porter, Amy Baltzell, Sarah Bergeron, Stephani Armitage-Johnson, Amy Fuller, and Stephanie Maxwell-Pierson saw the most racing action. During the first four rounds, the afterguard was generally composed of JJ Isler as the starting helmsman, who became tactician and turned the wheel over to Leslie Egnot after the start. Courtenay Becker-Dey was the navigator.

Studying the ESPN tapes helped Susie Leech Nairn win the bow position, and Merritt

Carey, fresh from the Whitbread, usually worked the sewer. Her height was a plus for Joan Touchette at the mast, and the experience in the pit benefited both Dawn Riley and Lisa Charles. Melissa Purdy was often found on the main, with Hannah Swett, Katie Pettibone, and Merritt Palm handling the trimming.

As injuries or exhaustion or excused absences opened up different positions, other team members were well practiced to stand in. Sue Dent, who began with the syndicate as a volunteer and was later invited to join the team because of her constant work and positive attitude, learned the bow position. Sarah Cavanagh worked the sewer, Diana Klybert's height benefited her in the mast position, and Linda Lindquist and Christy Evans were most often found in the pit. Anna Seaton Huntington and Suzette Hau'oli Smith were grinders, Debbie Pettibone was prepared to step in as a trimmer, and Annie Nelson worked as navigator.

It was often said by observers of both the '92 men's team and the '95 women's team that the women bonded together as a team much quicker than the men's team and that the women tended to view each individual more as a team member than as someone on the A or B team.

In the week before the historical first race of the 1995 defender races, only the weather got more attention than the women's team. A series of cold fronts brought heavy winds and rain, causing huge ocean swells, and even generating a mini-tornado that damaged PACT '95's boat, *Young America*. All this disrupted the scheduled opening round. The race scheduled for January 12 was cancelled and it wasn't until 12:45 P.M. on Friday the 13th that

America[3]—The Women's Team met Team Dennis Conner (TDC) at the starting line for the beginning of the Citizen Cup.

In winds of six to eight knots and seas of four to seven feet, the women aboard *America*[3] had to have their hearts in their throats as they entered into prestart maneuvers against the most experienced America's Cup team in San Diego, knowing that the entire sailing world was watching. Dennis Conner,

The racing yachts of the three defenders sail along San Diego's waterfront.

59

*(right, below
and right page)
Defender racing action in
the first three round-robins.*

"Mr. America's Cup," was at the helm of *Stars & Stripes,* and JJ Isler drove *America³.* Whether it was adrenaline, nerves, natural aggression, or just plain smart sailing, the women went right for the jugular at the first opportunity they had. With *America³* on starboard and owning right-of-way over their port-tack opponent, Isler drove straight at

Conner as the two yachts converged. Conner was obliged to keep clear, but the on-the-water umpires penalized him for not doing so soon enough, forcing *Stars & Stripes* into a 270-degree penalty turn immediately following the start.

As Isler handed the wheel to Egnot, the Conner team completed the penalty turn and the chase was on. Trailing by as many as ten lengths, there was little *Stars & Stripes* could do other than initiate a tacking duel, but Conner's new boat showed no appreciable speed advantage over the 1992 Cup victor, and the first leg of the first race in the first America's Cup in which a women's team competed went to *America³* by an insurmountable one minute and forty seconds. Over the next five legs the women maintained their lead by positioning their boat well, maintaining a loose

several tactical errors. Even so, the race was close for the first four legs until the wind dropped to four knots on the third beat and *Stars & Stripes*, designed for lighter air, gained more than seven minutes on that leg alone.

The toughest loss of the first round was against PACT '95 in the women's third race. With 1992 Olympic silver medalist Kevin Mahaney at the helm, the Roy Lichtenstein mermaid-painted *Young America* took the start, then added to her lead by protecting the favored left side of the course. But Egnot, steering *America³*, took advantage of an opportunity to position her yacht to the left of her opponent, an opportunity that gained her the lead. Once ahead, the team performed well and remained ahead until the fifth leg, when they were penalized for tacking too close. *Young America* regained the lead during the penalty turn and crossed the finish line thirty-seven seconds ahead.

Early round action between America³ *and* Young America *as the two racing yachts cut through waves off Point Loma.*

cover when necessary, and near flawless crew work. History records the final delta at 1:09, while headlines across the world proclaimed that the women were for real.

If emotions soared after that first race, they were quickly brought down to earth the following day. *America³* suffered a 5:47 trouncing after Conner gained the controlling position at the start and forced the women into

On deck crew work improved daily as the team became increasingly familiar with the size of the boat and the intricacies of the maneuvers.

The first round-robin ended with PACT '95 establishing a convincing lead over both Team Dennis Conner and A^3. The group from Maine collected five points, while Conner had three and America^3 tallied one.

It was after the first round that the coaching staff at America^3 decided changes were in order. The inexperience of the team was glaringly apparent. A problem that had plagued the team from the start was now becoming an ever-growing obstacle to winning. While the team seemed unified, there was no clear-cut leader; no one had stood up to take command. This may have been partially the result of the women becoming too reliant on the male coaches, and it may have been the natural result of the psychological makeup of the team. Whatever, it was decided that rotating Egnot and Riley at the helm, as had been done in the first round, would be scrapped in favor of placing Egnot behind the wheel on a permanent basis and making Riley the crew boss.

"We need Dawn to help out all over the boat," was the way Worthington evaluated the situation. Riley was clearly the most experienced sailor, with one America's Cup and two Whitbreads behind her, and she was also the

The strength of the women's team was questioned when first announced, but the argument fell silent once the grinders and trimmers proved their worth.

The grinders were always ready with a helping hand–ragged or not.

voice that the team listened to most when decisions on board had to be made. While she was positioned in the pit, she roamed the boat advising, suggesting, cajoling, ordering. She knew what needed to be done and she needed to assume the leadership role. Dick Dent said it best when asked what the changes would mean. "Dawn is like E. F. Hutton," said the trainer. "When she speaks, the team listens. There's never any second-guessing. She gives an order and it's done without reservation because everyone on the boat respects her and looks up to her."

The changes didn't sit well with everyone. Riley herself was quietly disappointed as she had hoped to helm the boat in the upcoming contests. It was somewhat ironic that she had been the one who encouraged Egnot to apply to A^3 in the first place. But

Riley respected Egnot's talents, and she obviously knew in the beginning that such a situation might occur.

While the mini shake-up probably brought the team together even closer as a unit, its desired effect was not registered in the win column in the second round of the series. Once again, the team won only one race, but

because of weather, two of the contests were cancelled. And, once again, the victory came in the first race of the round. This time, Mahaney and *Young America* were to the stern of *America³* as the women crossed the finish line.

In an exciting race which featured both mishaps and excellent tactical calls to catch windshifts, the women were buried at the start by a twenty-seven-second deficit, but fought back with the help of a favorable windshift to round the first windward mark in the lead by forty seconds, an impressive gain on the leg of 1:07. *Young America* came roaring back on the run to close within a boat length at the leeward mark, but then trouble with the gennaker take-down all but brought the boat to standstill. As

the wind increased and a dense fog bank rolled in, *America³* pulled out to a 1:19 lead on the third leg, trimmed to forty-six seconds by Mahaney and group on the fourth leg. Then, after the mark rounding, *America³* caught the spinnaker takedown problems that plagued *Young America* after leg two, and the women lost their lead, but gained it back by catching a shift on the left side of the course. The final run saw *Young America* closing fast, but not fast enough to overcome the fourteen-second delta at the finish line.

None of A³'s three losses in this round were blowouts, although a check of the final deltas might indicate otherwise. The 3:02 delta posted by PACT '95 in the teams' second

Crewmembers position themselves around the spinnaker pole, prepared for the next maneuver.

confrontation in the round doesn't account for the six lead changes in the race. The 4:45 winning time turned in by *Stars & Stripes* in their second match in the round with *America³* covers up the fact that during the first four legs, the women never trailed by more than four boat lengths. The big gains were made on significant windshifts that favored the men.

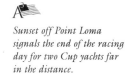

Sunset off Point Loma signals the end of the racing day for two Cup yachts far in the distance.

Although the women were continuing to prove that they were competitive, even if their score didn't necessarily confirm it, it was apparent that the new boats being raced by their two opponents were faster than *America³*. This did not come as a surprise to the syndicate's brain trust. A new-boat strategy had long been in place, based on a number of factors. Once Koch decided that the fund-raising had reached a level which would support the design and construction of a new boat, the question of timing became the major focus of the strategy team. It was a difficult decision. The longer the design and technology teams had to test and theorize and experiment, the better the chances for a major breakthrough. On the other hand, the longer

America³'s new boat gets loaded onto a Russian Antonov transport plane for its trip to San Diego.

the women's team sailed without the new boat, the less time they would have to get used to it, tune it, and learn to sail it to its optimum.

Because the first two round-robins afforded only one and two points per win, they were viewed more as training races than as critical point-winning opportunities. With four points per win at stake in round-robin three and seven points in round-robin four, it was obvious that the latter races became more important, but since all three teams were assured entry into the semifinals, it was during that mid-March series that the teams wanted to be at their peak.

Taking all that into consideration, it was decided to bring the new boat into service at the start of the fourth round-robin. So for round-robin three, *America³* was once more pressed into action. And once again, the women won the first race of the round, this time leading all the way for a 1:26 decision over TDC. The rest of the round went the way the rest of rounds one and two went, without

America³ finishing first again. But in a round that saw *Stars & Stripes* lose to *Young America* by an incredible 8:35 and win against the same boat by one second, the women's team was once again in every race, keeping each of the deltas but one around a minute.

As the third round was being raced, the new boat was completed at Eric Goetz Custom Sailboats in Bristol, Rhode Island. Towards the end of February, the boat was loaded onto a

Vincent Moeyersoms unwraps the new racer.

(right)
Prince Michael of Kent sitting with the former governor of Kansas, Joan Finney (second from left).

(below and right page) The christening of Mighty Mary *was cause for celebration.*

68

Russian Antonov cargo plane and flown to San Diego. After she was unwrapped and set up for racing, the team sailed her for a week before she was named during the March 1 christening ceremony.

"This boat is a tribute to human spirit," announced Bill Koch in front of some fifteen hundred invited guests. "It is an instrument of change. And it is being given to you women throughout the world. It is also a tribute to the woman who had the greatest effect on my life. That woman was my mother. And her nickname was 'Mighty Mary.'"

And so the new boat now carried the nickname and the legacy of Mary Koch.

The following day, March 2, *Mighty Mary* made her debut against *Stars & Stripes* in the first race of the fourth round. But, unlike each of the first races in the preceding rounds, the women were unable to find the finish line first. As Egnot later put it, the new boat experienced "teething problems," which began with a forty-five-minute postponement of the race while the steering system was adjusted. A temporary fix got her to the starting line, but problems with the steering cable persisted throughout the race. The spinnaker pole also presented difficulties. Still, the boat gave indications that once she was tuned and error-free, her speed would be apparent. At no point did she trail by more than four boat lengths, and the final delta was just 23 seconds.

The rest of the round showed considerable improvement. In her second race, *Mighty Mary* dusted *Young America* by fifty-six seconds after taking the start and leading at every mark. Her next race was on the day that will forever live in America's Cup history as the most tragic in the event's 144-year history—it

The state flower of Kansas, the sunflower, adorned the rear deck of the new America³ boat

(right page)
The beauty of sail is captured on a downwind leg as spinnaker are silhouetted on an azure sea.

Mighty Mary *sits in her cradle, hoping for gold at the end of the rainbow.*

was the day *oneAustralia* sank. With winds gusting to more than twenty knots and seas severely confused, the racing committee's decision to run the races will no doubt forever be questioned. Before the start on the defender's course, *Stars & Stripes* needed a postponement because of gear breakage. As the postponement time ran out, repairs were incomplete, and just after starting, *Stars & Stripes* was forced to drop her mainsail due to further equipment breakage. Crewman Ralf Steitz was sent up the mast to disengage the halyard lock, and while descending, he lost his grip and was flung behind the boat, catching himself on the

On the same day that the
Australian yacht sank,
Stars & Stripes *crewman
Ralf Steitz hung upside
down off the masthead
after losing his footing.*

74

backstay, where he hung suspended upside down for several minutes before bowman Greg Prussia climbed the mast to come to his aid. Conner and his team continued for two legs before retiring, and the victory went to *Mighty Mary*, but not before suffering some structural damage as well.

With the final three days of racing in the round cancelled due to winds either too light or too heavy, A^3 finished round-robin four with two wins and two losses and a total of twenty-one points. PACT '95 advanced to the semifinals in first place and thus carried the two bonus points into the series, while Team Dennis Conner carried forward one point, due to its second-place finish.

The break between the last round-robin and the semifinals was a time of some anguish and soul-searching in the America³ camp. With just five victories in the twenty races in which they'd competed, the women's team was searching for answers. They had only eight

Shot from a helicopter, the team is shown in position as the seas part and the sails strain against the wind.

Mighty Mary *in profile, racing against Dennis Conner's* Stars & Stripes.

whether or not they had the depth of tactical experience necessary to pull off what appeared to be a very formidable task. There was also a realization by some of the sailors and shoreside teams that the crew was not sailing the boat to its full potential. There was a growing belief that a good deal of speed in the boat had yet to be found. Several team members approached the coaches and management team, requesting a change in the afterguard that might provide them with more experience.

The solution was to replace JJ Isler with Dave Dellenbaugh, a controversial move that ended the all-female makeup of the racing squad and caused a brief uproar in the media

The bow of "the mermaid" cuts into the Pacific, somewhat obscuring the Roy Lichtenstein painted hull of the PACT '95 racer.

scheduled races left to beat out one of their two opponents in order to advance to the defender finals. They believed they had the boat that could do it in *Mighty Mary,* but there were questions among the women as to

and among some sponsors and some members of the public. But the change was made with the full support of the team and it was soon endorsed by most observers who realized that the possibility of winning the America's Cup was more important than repeatedly making a statement for gender equality.

Dellenbaugh seemed the perfect choice to step on board. His soft-spoken, mild manner coupled with his obvious intelligence and knowledge of the sport had won him respect and acceptance among the women. The team

had suggested that if someone was to be added to the afterguard, it should be Dellenbaugh. He assumed the role of tactician and starting helmsman, the dual roles he performed for the victorious 1992 team.

In his first start in the 1995 series, in the first race of the semifinals, Dellenbaugh gained the controlling position in the prestart maneuvering and crossed the line at the favored end. When the boats converged, Egnot was at the wheel and *Mighty Mary* was ahead. But with about one-third of the first leg left to sail, the

Dave Dellenbaugh was put on board at the start of the semifinals and acted as starting helmsman and tactician.

Two views of Mighty Mary *as she races for history and glory.*

wind dropped to about four knots and the "mostly" women's team, as the press now dubbed it, suffered through a slow tack that gave *Young America* the lead. Mahaney and crew rounded the first three marks ahead, but *Mighty Mary* gained on each leg until they were less than two boat lengths behind. A ripped gennaker on leg four spelled disaster for Dellenbaugh's debut, although *Mighty Mary* showed her speed with a gain of fifty-three seconds on the final run. It was impressive, but it wasn't enough, as *Young America* won by thirty-two seconds.

Mighty Mary's first semifinals victory came in its next race when the A[3] team put

Maintenance was part of the every day routine and no one was spared.

together near flawless tactics and boat handling to beat *Stars & Stripes* by 1:36. Dellenbaugh got the jump on his '92 competitor, Paul Cayard, at the start. Egnot, the crew, and *Mighty Mary* took over from there. With an eight-second lead over the start line, the team added gains on every leg until they rounded the second leeward mark with 2:10 separating the two boats. The final two legs were sailed

Courage, daring, and the skills of a trapeze preformer came in handy when climbing the mast was necessary.

Chubasco, *the team's tender, supply craft, spectator lanch, and all-round vessel was ever-present whenever the team was racing or training.*

On-the-water umpiring helped adjudicate some rules violations immediately, but there was still much time spent in the jury room ashore.

safely and conservatively, giving America[3] the point and evening the points total with Team Dennis Conner.

From that point on, PACT '95 ran away with the series. Winning each of its first four contests and adding on the two bonus points they received for their round-robin success, the syndicate based in Maine mathematically

clinched a place in the defender finals. This left America[3] and TDC in a ferocious battle for the other spot.

But just at the point that one would think the outcome of the semifinals would result from the action at sea, the real story of the series began to take shape on land. It all began halfway up the second beat in race eight of the semis when *Stars & Stripes* came perilously close to dropping their keel in their race versus *Young America*. Damage to the keelbox area resulted in the keel being replaced. The following day, A[3] beat PACT '95 in a race with four lead changes to once again even the score with Team Dennis Conner.

While *Mighty Mary* and *Young America* were tangling on the racecourse, a new keel was fitted onto *Stars & Stripes*, which prompted the America[3] team to fly a red technical protest flag in their race the next day against

Susie Nairn works the bow as Mighty Mary *leads* Young America *in a close race.*

Team Dennis Conner. The victory went to *Stars & Stripes* in a race in which they led at every mark, but A[3] protested, claiming the keel change was made during a "no-change" period and thus was illegal. The case went to the international jury, but no decision was reached until all racing in the semifinals had been completed. At that point, America[3] and TDC were tied with three points each, pending the protest. In the eight races both teams competed in, America[3] had scored three victories, and Conner's team had two wins and the one-point carryover from the round-robins.

During the hearing, America[3] learned that measurers had disallowed the change, but political maneuvering by Team Dennis Conner convinced a friendly defense committee to overrule the measurers, contrary to established rules. Then the jury issued a curious decision. It upheld the protest by America[3], "annulled" Team Dennis Conner's win, and ordered a resail of the race. As team captain Dawn Riley said in a press conference: "We are confused with the remedy for this infringement. If Team Dennis Conner's keel was ruled illegal for Tuesday's race and we properly finished, we should be awarded the point since *Mighty Mary* was the only legal boat on the water."

While that argument made good sense, the history of the America's Cup has often proved that logic has little bearing on official decisions. Yet had the jury ruled to either strip Conner of his point or award the race to A[3], the women's team would have advanced to the finals then and there. Instead, it all came down to the sail-off—if *Mighty Mary* won, she would advance; if not, there would be yet another sail-off.

The headlines for the sail-off read: "*Stars & Stripes* Wins, *Mighty Mary* Over Early." Little more needs to be said. The bow of USA-43 inched over the start line a fraction too soon and by the time the team jibed back and restarted, they trailed by fifty-three seconds. The final delta was a maddening 4:55.

That set up what pundits began calling "the sail of the century," but it turned out to be a meaningless exercise. Unbeknownst to the women's team, the three defense syndicates had met deep into the early morning hours of the race day and had cut a deal under which all three teams would advance to the finals. Three

boats in a two-boat final stretched credibility, but then, as stated, logic often plays no part in such decisions.

Unfortunately for America[3], they put together one of their best races of the defender trials and demolished *Stars & Stripes* by nearly six minutes. Believing they had earned

Bill Koch and John Marshall shake on "the deal" that placed all three defenders in the finals. Dennis Conner looks on.

Fast hands and strength are key to gathering a mountain of spinnaker material before it drops into the sea.

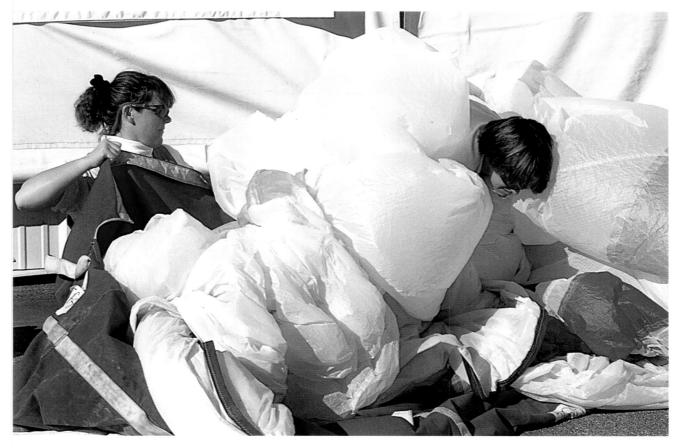

Mighty Mary was named in honor of Bill Koch's mother, a woman known for her skill and competitiveness in several sports.

an entry into the finals against PACT '95, the team celebrated in pure joy until they were informed of "the deal." Still, they were advancing to the finals, although this new series amounted to a replay of the semifinals.

But the replay was anything but that for PACT '95. Having secured their finals spot very early in the semis, why they consented to "the deal" became the question most asked by Cup observers. In the end, it gave Dennis Conner new life, something Cup history had

shown almost always worked in his favor. It was not for nothing that he was often called "The Comeback Kid."

By the time each of the three teams had completed four races in the finals, they were all tied with three points each, although their number of victories were not equal. PACT '95 had won only one of its races, but having carried over two points from their first-place finish in the semis, they stood equal with their two opponents. America[3] had beat PACT '95 on the first day of the finals and had given TDC its only loss to date on race day six.

At the end of race day nine, with just two races left to sail, America[3] was on the brink of elimination. Conner had now notched five wins in six races and led the series with five points. Both PACT '95 and America[3] had posted two victories, leaving the women's team with just three points and the men from Maine with four. One more loss for America[3] would bring its historic quest to an end.

But America[3] fought back to take a critical race off PACT '95, tying them at four points each. Both teams would race TDC one

Vincent Moeyersoms briefs the team as rules advisor Barbara Farquhar and syndicate chairman Bill Kock look on.

more time to decide who would advance into the America's Cup match against the challenger.

After *Young America* beat *Stars & Stripes* in its final scheduled race, the scores were now five points each for PACT '95 and TDC and four points for America[3]. So it all came down to the final race between TDC and A[3]. If TDC won, they'd race in the Cup. If A[3] won, TDC would be eliminated based on the previously agreed-upon format and A[3] would race a sail-off with PACT '95. Outside of the team itself, not many sailboat-racing fans had truly believed a year earlier that the women's team would be in this position at the end of April 1995.

The final race has been termed the most incredible result in the history of the America's Cup. It was an unbelievable win for Dennis Conner's team and an absolute heartbreaker for the women's team. In eight knots of wind, nerves were evident at the start as both boats crossed the line early. Dellenbaugh, however, was very close to the line and quickly cleared. Cayard had less speed and was forced to jibe back, a maneuver that cost him twenty-four seconds.

USA-43 extended its lead through flawless crew work and being favored by several windshifts. By leg four, the breeze was dying, but *Mighty Mary* rounded the second leeward mark with what seemed to be an insurmountable 3:31 lead. The team stretched that to 4:08 at the last windward mark and now had only to successfully negotiate the final run to force the sail-off with *Young America*.

And then the wheels came off. As the breeze dropped off even more, both boats had rounded and set asymmetrical gennakers, but the two teams headed for different sides of the course. *Mighty Mary* sailed into a hole with little or no air, while *Stars & Stripes* picked up a different breeze and more pressure, allowing TDC to halve the lead. The bad luck aboard *Mighty Mary* was followed by several bad jibes during a Cayard-initiated jibing duel that allowed *Stars & Stripes* to close the gap and eventually roll over the struggling *Mighty Mary*. With less than a half mile to the finish line, TDC overtook USA-43 and sailed themselves into the America's Cup.

Sailor's are a superstitious lot. Here Leslie Egnot hangs a good-luck feather below decks.

Much has been written and speculated about that last race in the defender finals. Armchair admirals have dissected leg six more times than any other single leg in any sailboat race ever sailed, and no unanimity of opinion has been reached. Was the loss of the enormous lead a result of bad tactics, bad crew work, or just bad luck? Should *Mighty Mary* have covered *Stars & Stripes* earlier? Could they have done so in the dying breeze? Was *Stars & Stripes* simply a faster boat in the very light air? Or did it all come down to the fact that TDC found wind when A³ didn't?

Whatever the answers, the fact remains that Dennis Conner once again found himself

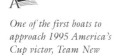

racing in an America's Cup match. And perhaps in keeping with the bizarre nature of the defender trials, he decided to discard his own boat and sail *Young America* against Team New Zealand, which had just completed an unprecedented sweep through the challenger ranks, posting but one loss over five months of racing.

The Kiwis continued their juggernaught with five straight wins over Dennis and his newly acquired mermaid. The comeback was incomplete.

Just as the discussion of that last leg will no doubt be fodder for barroom and yacht club conversations for years to come, so, too,

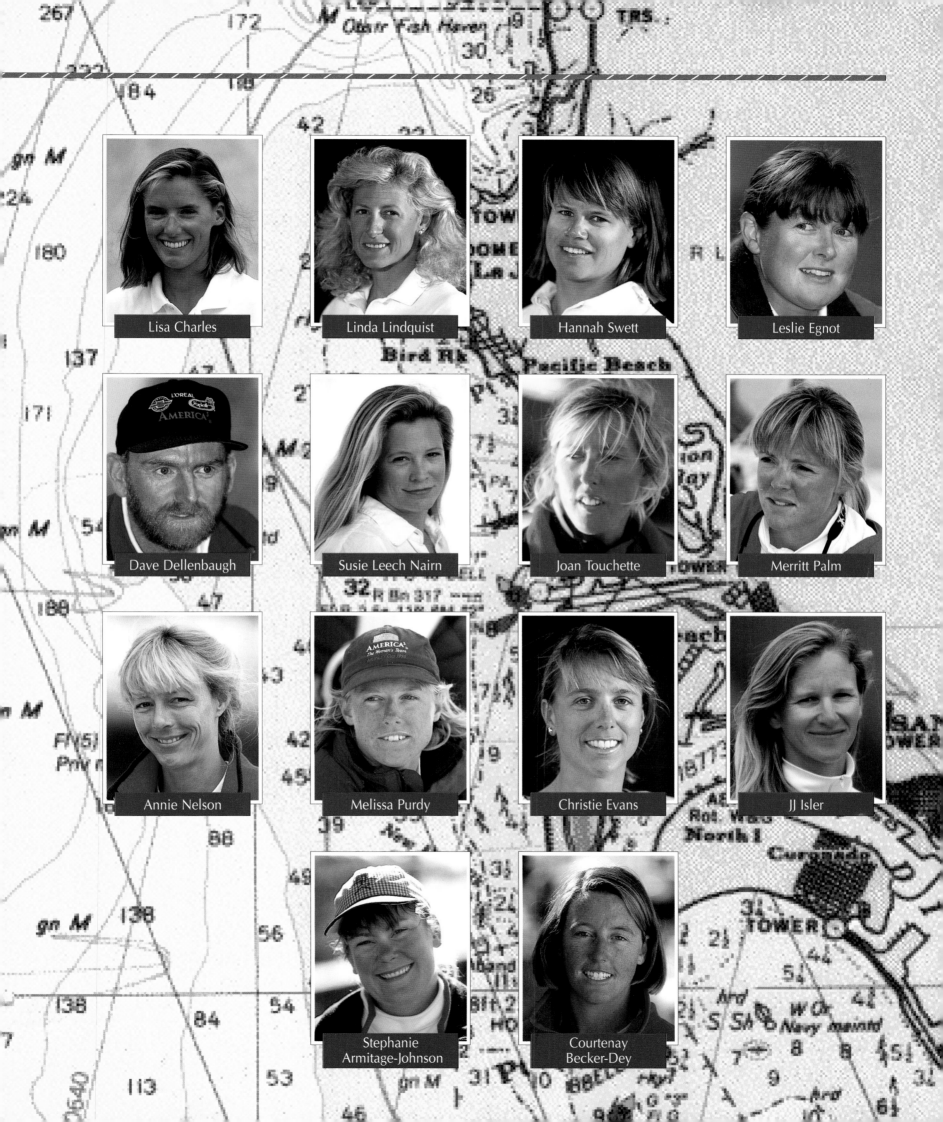

Lisa Charles

Linda Lindquist

Hannah Swett

Leslie Egnot

Dave Dellenbaugh

Susie Leech Nairn

Joan Touchette

Merritt Palm

Annie Nelson

Melissa Purdy

Christie Evans

JJ Isler

Stephanie
Armitage-Johnson

Courtenay
Becker-Dey

TEAMMATES

Walter Cooper
and Debbie Pettibone

Barbara Farquhar

Jim Cronin

Susan Daly

Mike Fiore, Buddy Melges,
and Phil Uhl

Jack Kleene

Margaret Mellin

Elva "Gigi" Pearse

Mary Chaundy

Hanna, Per, Candace, and
Matilda Andersson

Amanda Russell
and Steve Harrison

Barbara Anderson

Janet Thompson

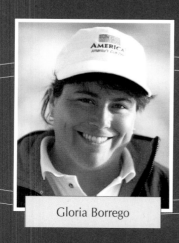

Gloria Borrego

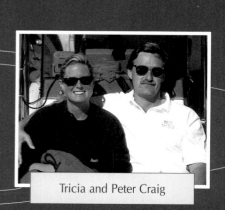

Tricia and Peter Craig

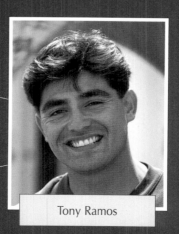

Tony Ramos

Gisela Garneau

Cynthia Boccara,
giving a massage

John Kolius

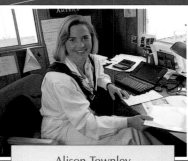

Alison Townley

Astrid, Vincent, and Acadia
Moeyersoms

Richard Callahan

Alison Hamilton

Thor Ramsing

Daniel Forster

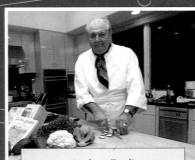

Andrea Dodi

Jon Mulligan, Carol Vernon,
and Diana Klybert

Suzanne Durette

Chubasco

Jennifer Kloos

Carol Vernon

Steve Connett

TEAMMATES

Mike Dailey

Dick Dent and Judy Robinson

Jerry Kirby

Sandra Bateman
and Will Robinson

Dennis Baxter

Veronica Cahill

Dirk Kramers

Susie Weaver

Sandy Worcester

Dave Frank and Rodney Ernst

Jeanne Kleene

Felix Gonzales

Hilary Christopher
and Kenya Williamson

Rick Wrightson

Sheila Roell

Phil Keester

Chris Ross

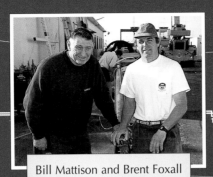

Bill Mattison and Brent Foxall

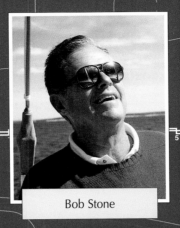

Bob Stone

Mark and Karen Richards

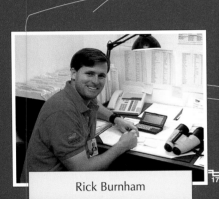

Rick Burnham

Ellen Bloom

Peter, Craig, and Pamela Julias

Brett Crawford

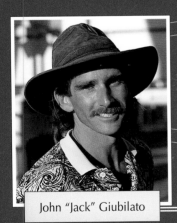

John "Jack" Giubilato

Kezia and Dave Disney

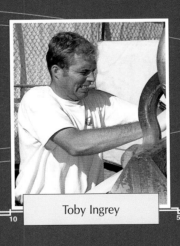

Toby Ingrey

Mike Kent

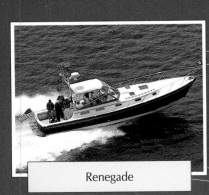

Renegade

Bob Campbell

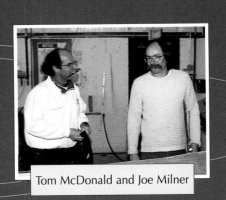

Tom McDonald and Joe Milner

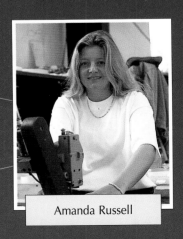

Amanda Russell

TEAMMATES

Fernando Frimm

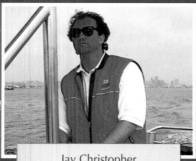

Jay Christopher

Dave Bieling

Sean Habgood

Mike and Lisa Eldred

Mark Curley

Greg (or Gary?) Pierson

Kimo Worthington

Mike Hein

Mark Irwin

Eduardo Guillergan

Daniel Forster, Jon Mulligan,
and Phil Uhl

Chris Crabtree

Buddy Melges

Jackie O'Dell

Jim Dey

Ned Chambers, M.D.

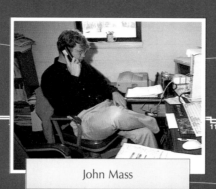

John Mass

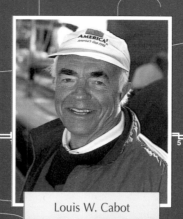

Louis W. Cabot

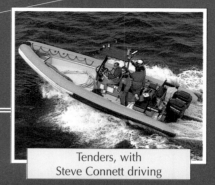

Tenders, with
Steve Connett driving

Dina Kowalyshin

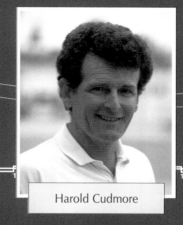

Harold Cudmore

Ed Frank

Paul Larsen

Stu Argo

(L to R) Front: Veronica Cahill, Susan Daly, Katie Worthington,
Tricia Craig Back: Kimoko Augustine, Suzanna Grubb,
Candace Andersson, Sheila Roell

David A. Rosow

Doug Augustine

Peter McCarthy

OFFICIAL RECORD OF THE
1995 AMERICA'S CUP DEFENDER RACES

ROUND ROBIN I

January 13 - January 22
1 point per win

Race 1 *America³* def *Stars & Stripes* by 1:16
Race 2 *Stars & Stripes* def *America³* by 5:47
Race 3 *Young America* def *America³* by 0:37
Race 4 *Young America* def *America³* by 3:32
Race 5 *Young America* def *Stars & Stripes* by 0:18
Race 6 *Young America* def *Stars & Stripes* by 5:00
Race 7 *Young America* def *America³* by 2:02
Race 8 *Stars & Stripes* def *America³* by 1:51
Race 9 *Stars & Stripes* def *America³* by 3:09

STANDINGS AFTER ROUND ROBIN I

Boat	W	L	Points
Young America	5	1	5
Stars & Stripes	3	3	3
America³	1	5	1

ROUND ROBIN II

January 29 - February 7
2 points per win

Race 1 *America³* def *Young America* by 0:14
Race 2 *Stars & Stripes* def *Young America* by DNF
Race 3 *Stars & Stripes* def *America³* by 1:29
Race 4 *Stars & Stripes* def *America³* by 4:45
Race 5 *Young America* def *Stars & Stripes* by 1:46
Race 6 *Stars & Stripes* def *America³* by 0:28
Race 7 *Young America* def *America³* by 3:02

STANDINGS AFTER ROUND ROBIN II

Boat	Round		Overall		
	W	L	W	L	Points
Young America	2	2	7	3	9
Stars & Stripes	3	1	6	4	9
America³	1	3	2	8	2

Note: Not all races in the round were scored due to weather

ROUND ROBIN III

February 15 - February 24
4 points per win

Race 1 *America³* def *Stars & Stripes* by 1:26
Race 2 *Young America* def *America³* by 1:20
Race 3 *Stars & Stripes* def *America³* by 1:08
Race 4 *Young America* def *Stars & Stripes* by 8:35
Race 5 *Young America* def *America³* by 2:24
Race 6 *Stars & Stripes* def *Young America* by 0:03
Race 7 *Stars & Stripes* def *Young America* by 1:33
Race 8 *Young America* def *America³* by 1:19
Race 9 *Stars & Stripes* def *America³* by 1:52

STANDINGS AFTER ROUND ROBIN III

Boat	Round		Overall		
	W	L	W	L	Points
Young America	4	2	11	5	25
Stars & Stripes	4	2	10	6	25
America³	1	5	3	13	7

ROUND ROBIN IV

March 2 - March 10
7 points per win

Race 1 *Stars & Stripes* def *Mighty Mary* by 0:23
Race 2 *Mighty Mary* def *Young America* by 0:56
Race 3 *Young America* def *Stars & Stripes* by 1:03
Race 4 *Mighty Mary* def *Stars & Stripes* by DNF
Race 5 *Young America* def *Mighty Mary* by 4:35
Race 6 *Young America* def *Stars & Stripes* by 2:06
Race 7 *Stars & Stripes* def *Mighty Mary* by 1:35
Race 8 *Young America* def *Mighty Mary* race
        abandoned

STANDINGS AFTER ROUND ROBIN IV

Boat	Round		Overall		
	W	L	W	L	Points
Young America	3	1	14	6	46
Stars & Stripes	1	3	11	9	32
Mighty Mary	2	2	5	15	21

Note: Not all races in the round were scored due to weather. *Mighty Mary* was substituted for *America³*. *Young America* earned two bonus points in semi-finals for winning round robin series and *Stars & Stripes* earned one bonus point in the semi-finals for placing second.

SEMI-FINALS		CITIZEN CUP FINALS	
March 18 - April 3		April 10 - April 26	

SEMI-FINALS

March 18 - April 3

Race 1   *Young America* def *Mighty Mary* by 0:32
Race 2   *Mighty Mary* def *Stars & Stripes* by 1:36
Race 3   *Young America* def *Stars & Stripes* by 0:28
Race 4   *Stars & Stripes* def *Mighty Mary* by DNF
Race 5   *Young America* def *Mighty Mary* by 0:47
Race 6   *Young America* def *Stars & Stripes* by DNF
Race 7   *Mighty Mary* def *Young America* by 0:38
Race 8   *Stars & Stripes* def *Mighty Mary* by 1:31*
Race 9   *Young America* def *Mighty Mary* by 1:44
Race 10   *Young America* def *Stars & Stripes* by 0:44
Race 11   *Mighty Mary* def *Stars & Stripes* by 2:04
Race 12   *Young America* def *Stars & Stripes* by 0:52
Race 13   *Stars & Stripes* def *Mighty Mary* by 4:49
Race 14   *Mighty Mary* def *Stars & Stripes* by 5:59

STANDINGS AFTER SEMI-FINALS

Boat	W	L
Young America	9	1
Mighty Mary	4	5
Stars & Stripes	3	7

* The international jury threw out race 8 due to *Stars & Stripes* sailing with an illegal modification.

Young America earned two bonus points for winning semi-finals. *Mighty Mary* earned one bonus point for placing second in semi-finals.

CITIZEN CUP FINALS

April 10 - April 26

Race 1   *Mighty Mary* def *Young America* by 0:48
Race 2   *Stars & Stripes* def *Young America* by 1:15
Race 3   *Stars & Stripes* vs *Mighty Mary* race abandoned
Race 4   *Stars & Stripes* def *Mighty Mary* by 2:50
Race 5   *Young America* def *Mighty Mary* by 1:24
Race 6   *Stars & Stripes* def *Young America* by 0:01
Race 7   *Mighty Mary* def *Stars & Stripes* by 0:41
Race 8   *Young America* def *Mighty Mary* by 2:46
Race 9   *Stars & Stripes* def *Young America* by 0:45
Race 10   *Stars & Stripes* def *Mighty Mary* by 1:02
Race 11   *Mighty Mary* def *Young America* by 1:08
Race 12   *Young America* def *Stars & Stripes* by 0:52
Race 13   *Stars & Stripes* def *Mighty Mary* by 0:52

STANDINGS AFTER CITIZEN CUP FINALS

Boat	W	L
Stars & Stripes	6	2
Young America	5	5
Mighty Mary	4	5

Stars & Stripes advances to America's Cup match versus Team New Zealand

INDEX

PHOTO CREDITS

Daniel Forster

Bob Greiser

Dan Nerney

Sharon Green

Matthew J. Atanian

Walter Cooper

Onne Van Der Wal

Bob Wolfe

and

Special Thanks to ACTV/PPL for Use of Their Videotape